No Ordinary Man

THE REMARKABLE LIFE OF
F. B. MEYER

By
W. Y. FULLERTON D.D.

AMBASSADOR

No Ordinary Man
F. B. Meyer

ISBN   0   907927   91   2

AMBASSADOR PRODUCTIONS LTD.,
Providence House,
16 Hillview Avenue,
Belfast, BT5 6JR,
U.K.

CONTENTS

INTRODUCTION

When I was a lad, one wet summer's afternoon, I lifted an auto-biography from my Aunt's bookshelf and got hooked on its contents. The book was called "My Pilgrimage" by F.W. Boreham and told the story of his fascinating life which stretched from being C.H. Spurgeon's last student to becoming a pastor in Australia and, arguably, the most popular Christian essayist of his day.

Boreham, I was to discover, was a Christian writer who believed people were better won with honey than vinegar and his books always had a gentle Christ exalting tone to them, drawn from stories of everyday life. I was to read most of them and to find them a very real help in my young Christian life.

Why, then, in this introduction to a life of F.B. Meyer, do I begin with Boreham? The answer is simple; it was Boreham who first introduced me to the writings of Meyer! He describes in his autobiography how he used to go to F.B. Meyer's Saturday afternoon Bible Class in London and how, though other preachers in that high Victorian day drew thousands to hear them, it was Meyer who got under his skin and gripped his heart. He notes that he never heard Meyer preach without feeling that, in a special way, he had been lifted nearer to God.

So it was that I was introduced to the man who inspired Boreham to live for God and who in turn, though being dead, was to deeply inspire me. In the gracious will of God I was called to establish a Bible Class with the Crescent Church in the University district of Belfast and have over these last, almost, 17 years, now, been faced with multitudes of lives who have poured out to listen, with hungry hearts, to God's Word expounded. I have found it a mammoth task to feel all these spiritually hungry lives, but also a deeply rewarding one. I want to acknowledge my deep indebtedness to F.B. Meyer for the help his writings have given me, time and again, as I have sought to apply the Scriptures to my own generation.

Meyer's expositions of the lives of Abraham, Jacob, Moses, Joseph, David, Samuel and other Bible characters helped me to see how practical the Scriptures are in the lessons they teach for everyday living. Meyer had a way of showing that the love of God is not determined by what it finds in us. I recall how he teaches that when Peter denied his Lord he was later amazed to discover that the Lord loved him still: neither Peter's sin, nor mood, nor temptation could staunch Christ's love and commitment to him.

Meyer's "Christ in Isaiah" is one of the most comforting books I have ever read: I have felt as close to the Saviour when reading Meyer's beautiful exposition of Isaiah's majestic chapters on the Messiah than at any other time in my life. In that he comforted me with his writing, I found that I was enabled by God to try to reach out and comfort others.

It was Meyer's writing ability that makes his books different. Good writing is a great gift and a rarity because a lot of Christian books are full of cliches and bland regurgitation. Meyer had an ear for poetry and his writing often reveals a great ability to write almost poetic prose in the service of Bible exposition. He is the Laurie Lee, even, in a sense, the Wordsworth or Betjeman of the evangelical world. He had a very observant eye for nature around him and his books are full of parables from rivers and trees and flowers and animals. He also had a very wide experience of how human beings behave and what motivates them. He was, of course a born romantic, and God knows such are, unfortunately, never thick on the ground at any time. You will find, if you are persuaded to read his works, which I hope you will be, that little phrases Meyer uses in his books will stay with you for years. Amazing it is to think that a lot of his works were written on trains as he travelled about the world on one of the busiest schedules, both nationally and internationally, any servant of God was ever called upon to carry through. To any person interested in the difficult task of making righteousness readable, Meyer is a starlight of encouragement who proves by the way he wrote that it can be done.

I also revere the memory of F.B. Meyer for his ability to attack error by teaching truth. This shows error up like nothing else does. He also has a commendable characteristic in that he does not spend his time cat calling those who differed with him, even in the Christian world. He had his enemies and many were jealous of his outstanding abilities, but, he knew he could afford to be magnanimous and he lets them go choosing to go for eternal themes which would outlast the yapping little dogs snapping at his heels. All of this becomes distilled nectar in his writing, for nothing is wasted and his works are as relevant to the human heart today as the day they were first written in those crowded railway carriages of the Victorian and Edwardian era!

Throughout all of my ministry I have often wondered what made the godly F.B. Meyer, tick. What life lay behind the five million copies of his books that sold during his lifetime? What drew great multitudes of people to listen to this gentle spiritual giant? What kind of preaching led to the Post Office at Keswick running out of postal orders the morning after Meyer had preached in the great Convention tent on the subject of holiness? The postal orders were taken up by Christians paying their bills the morning after the night before! What quality of man inspired the congregation at his funeral service to sing the "Hallelujah Chorus"?

Fullerton's fascinating and most readable life of F.B. Meyer answered these questions for me. It is my prayer that it will answer the same question for you. Here is a book which glows with touching and very moving stories of a life lived to God's glory. I am convinced it will be a blessing to a new generation facing the problems of a new century with the same Saviour as F.B. Meyer's in their hearts.

Derick Bingham
Belfast

September, 1993

CHAPTER ONE

GROWTH INTO MANHOOD

THE first glimpse we have into the soul of F. B. Meyer is his mother's record that when he was about five years of age, he added to his regular prayers one Sunday evening the petition, " Put Thy Holy Spirit in me to make my heart good, like Jesus Christ was," and thereafter continued to say it every day. The last glimpse was given the day before he died, when, in response to a question as to whether he then had any new vision of his Saviour, looking upward he simply said, " No, just the constant interchange between Him and me." Interchange—the word is worthy of remembrance—not prayer only, nor only worship, but fellowship, the speech of the heart and the response of the Spirit. Between those two experiences his whole life was included ; the final witness was the answer to the early wish ; there was no need of ecstasy at the end nor place for it ; as he lived he died. Christ and he were well known to each other.

He was born on April 8th, 1847, and departed on March 28th, 1929, the very day on which, before his illness, he had arranged to start for a great journey. He had in mind Canada and California, but God had prepared some better thing for him ; the date in his diary was right, the destination was wrong. Almost eighty-two years of age, full of faith and of good works he passed over, and doubtless " all the trumpets sounded for him on the other side." There were seventy-seven years between his early prayer and his latest testimony ; sixty years between the beginning of his ministry and the end of it.

Other men had perhaps greater natural qualities, but it is probably true that when he died there was no man of his day who had won such a wealth of affection. His own estimate of himself and his powers was simple and un-affected, though unduly modest. " I am only an ordinary man," he said. " I have no special gifts. I am no orator, no scholar, no profound thinker. If I have done anything for Christ and my generation, it is because *I have given myself entirely to Christ Jesus, and then tried to do whatever He wanted me to do.*" And is not that the invariable road to spiritual power ? To possess the Pearl of Great Price the seeker must sell all that he hath to purchase it ; the price varies, but it is never less than All.

Never less. Florence Nightingale said, " If I could give you the story of my life, it would be to show how one woman of ordinary ability " (here we are reminded of Meyer) " has been led by God in strange and unaccustomed paths to do in His name what He has done in her. And, if I could tell you all, you would see how God has done all and I nothing. I have worked very hard, that is all, and *I have never refused God anything.*" Change only the names and the spheres and in the mouth of two witnesses the thing is established. The dream is doubled because the interpretation thereof is sure.

Jean Ingelow has truly said that " Our only greatness is that we aspire." F. B. Meyer always aspired ; that which was true of John Richard Green as inscribed on his tomb at Mentone, was also true of him, " He died learning," and it might well be his epitaph too. At the funeral service beside the grave in Bournemouth, so beautifully situated, it was suggested that an appropriate record would be " Here lies a man that reckoned on God." At various times he himself hinted at two mottoes : one—" The man that had two talents came " ; the other—" John did no miracle, but all that he spake of This Man was true " : both revealing his humble estimate of himself.

The first of his family was from Germany. John Sebastian

Meyer came from Worms to London in the early part of the eighteenth century, bringing with him suggestions of Luther from his native city, and of Bach, whose first names—John Sebastian—he bore in memory of the friendship between his family and the great composer. He was a sugar refiner ; his son George was partner in a flourishing City firm, and his grandson Frederick a successful merchant. It is interesting to note that this Meyer attended Charlotte Chapel, Edinburgh, in his student days. He married a daughter of Henry Sturt, whose mother, Ann, a remarkable woman, was excommunicated from the Society of Friends because she was married in Lambeth Parish Church. Frederick Brotherton Meyer was therefore the great-grandson of John Sebastian Meyer, the grandson of George Meyer, the only son of Frederick Meyer. He was the inheritor of the characteristics of his ancestors, especially of the Quaker simplicity of his grandmother, whose literary tastes seemed also to be reproduced in her grandson. His second name was given in honour of a noted friend of the family, a member of the Parliament of that day, a statue of whom is in Peel Park, Salford. Fuller family details can be found in the memoir, " F. B. Meyer : His Life and Work," by M. Jennie Street, which was published a quarter of a century ago. Enough is written here to show that Dr. Meyer had the blessing of good ancestry, blood ran pure in his veins, and there can be little doubt that this, in considerable measure, accounted for the endurance and fortitude of his long life.

The family, who lived at Clapham Common, attended Bloomsbury Chapel, that great centre of usefulness in the heart of London, then under the famous ministry of Dr. Brock. On Sunday evenings the boy would, like many other boys, preach in the dining room. On one of these occasions the lad said something that led one of the housemaids to turn to Christ, and quite early in his life the desire grew in his heart to be a minister of the Gospel. At first his mother taught him at home, then he went to a preparatory school, and when in 1855 the family removed to Brighton he became after a while a student in Brighton College. Here he had to endure the usual " ragging," and on one occasion only escaped his tormentors by promising to do what they demanded—bring them some foreign stamps the following day. He had no idea where he would get them, scarcely knew what foreign stamps were, but he prayed for the stamps, passed a sleepless night, and just before starting for school summoned up courage to ask his father if he had any. To his surprise his father turned out a packet of letters that had just arrived from abroad, gave him the stamps, and sent him in triumph to conciliate his tormentors and gain the respect of the school.

Unforeseen business difficulties brought the family back to London. While staying with his uncle, Mr. George Gladstone, at Clapham, until such time as the new home was settled at Streatham, the growing lad then attended a school at Denmark Hill. Mr. J. T. Howieson, who was a junior in the same school at the same time, describes him then " as having the complexion a girl might have envied. He was dubbed ' The Rosy Meyer ' and was, I imagine, like David at the same age, ruddy and withal of a beautiful countenance and goodly to look on." New Park Road Chapel then became the spiritual home of the family, and on June 2nd, 1864, Frederick was there baptized on confession of faith by the pastor, Rev. David Jones, who afterwards became his fast friend.

While at Brighton the Meyers attended the ministry of Wade Robinson, the poet preacher, who exerted a lasting influence on the boy in his early teens. The tenor of his teaching may be guessed from his hymns, by which, more than by his sermons, the preacher will be remembered. It was he who gave to the world that verse so frequently quoted by those who have experienced the transforming power of grace :

> Heaven above is softer blue,
>   Earth around is sweeter green !
> Something lives in every hue
>   Christless eyes have never seen :

Birds with gladder songs o'erflow,
Flowers with deeper beauties shine,
Since I knew as now I know,
I am His, and He is mine.

The hymn moves on to its climax, one of the most triumphant expressions of faith ever penned or sung, and we may believe the truth of it was sung into the soul of young Meyer.

Heaven and Earth may fade and flee,
First-born light in gloom decline,
But while God and I shall be,
I am His and He is mine.

He had long been haunted with the impression that he was destined to be a minister of the Gospel, an impression which was deepened when one Sunday morning, on the way out from the service at Bloomsbury, Dr. Brock, who stood near the door, laid his hand on his shoulder and ventured on a prophecy. " Some day," he said, " *you* will be a minister, and stand at the end of the aisle, and shake hands with the people as I am doing now."

" At sixteen," he says, " the secret was still locked in my breast, but a matter of very serious and incessant debate. I had been pleading with tears and cries that God would show me His will, and especially that He would give me some assurance as to my powers of speech. Turning to my Bible, it fell open at the first chapter of Jeremiah and I saw the seventh verse, which I had never seen before. With indescribable feelings I read it again and again, and even now never come on it without a thrill of emotion. It was the answer to all my perplexing questionings. Yes, I was the child : I was to go to those to whom He sent me and speak what He bade me : He would be with me and touch my lips."

On March 14th, 1864, he wrote definitely expressing his dependence on God and giving reasons why he wished to be a preacher ; and on April 4th emphasised in a letter his purpose which had been strengthened by some sign he had sought from God, something like Gideon's sign of the dew on the fleece and on the floor—a somewhat precarious guidance had it not been strengthened by a growing assurance that this way lay God's will, and an evident and maturing fitness for the sacred office.

One Sunday evening, when his mother, to whom he had already opened his mind, had retired to rest, he remained behind, and " with great modesty and deep feeling," as his father records, " introduced the subject of his future." His father's treatment of him reveals such rare wisdom and true sympathy that any son might be proud to have had such a father, who writes of his boy, " With tears and faltering speech, and the most touching expressions of unfitness, except as the Holy Spirit made him fit for the work, he expressed the inward workings of his mind. I confess I felt abashed before the simple faith of my boy and cheerfully approved his decision, and commended him to our Heavenly Father's guidance and loving care."

This was just before he was seventeen years old, and on his seventeenth birthday, when out driving with his mother, he spoke to her of his decision. She quite properly reminded him of the apparent sacrifice of worldly prospects he was about to make, and, while consenting, ventured to suggest that if after a fair trial for a few years he wished to change, it would be possible. On which he looked at his mother very straitly and said, " Never ! That would be putting my hand to the plough and looking back."

Very wisely his parents decided that whether he was to be a minister or not he should have some experience of business life. It would be a distinct advantage if every candidate for the ministry had touch with the rough and tumble of the men who sit in the pews or leave the Churches severely alone. Mr. W. T. Stead, in one of his whimsical moments, declared that every minister should first of all serve as a policeman for a year, just to learn something of the underside of life from which he is afterwards to endeavour to win men and women.

Nothing quite so drastic was attempted in the Meyer household, but the son, having declared his intention, was tested and trained by two years' experience in the office of tea merchants in Billiter Square. Morning by morning he journeyed from Streatham to London Bridge by rail and crossed the bridge on foot to his business appointment. He often spoke of his wonder when one morning he heard the waves against the bridge, and realised that Father Thames is always singing, wonder that he had passed over the bridge so often and had not heard it, wonder at the sweetness of the lapping wavelets of which he was conscious for the first time. The roar of the city traffic had hitherto deadened the sound, and when he recalled the incident later and referred to the undertones of life, it carried the lesson home forcefully to busy men. He himself was diligent in business during those two years, tea-sampling and tea-tasting as well as book-keeping and invoicing— a discipline that stood him in good stead in the after years when he became known for his practical methods and unfailing punctuality.

During these years he took frequent part in a debating society, seized every available opportunity of hearing such preachers as were masters of their art—Landels, Binney, Parker and Spurgeon. At Pembury, near Tunbridge Wells, on one of his visits to an uncle who lived there, he first preached when he was sixteen years of age, his text being " The Lord will give grace and glory." In the following year his minister arranged some preaching engagements for him, and in 1866 he preached in various mission halls, was approved by his pastor and by Dr. Brock, applied for admission to Regent's Park College, passed a preliminary examination in June and entered in October.

A bundle of letters has been found amongst Dr. Meyer's effects, which he wrote to some friend whom he addressed as Herbert, evidently much valued by his correspondent, and probably returned to their writer when Herbert had passed out of this life. There is no clue in the letters to the identity of his correspondent, and many of the letters are undated, though they evidently range from 1865 to 1868. but Mr. Meyer's sisters, who still live at Pembury, recall that his name was Herbert Allport. Some are addressed from the Streatham home, some from Regent's Park College. There seems at one time to have been a sustained argument about the Gospel between the two. Meyer's handwriting changed during these years from the spidery scrawl of the boy to the round hand so often seen in later life, an evidence, I suggest, of enlarging character.

It is only possible to give the merest extracts from these epistles, even that, perhaps, scarcely necessary. Here are some samples :—

" If you want to hear a very sarcastic, withering, powerful sermon, go and hear Mursell, Clapham Road, Sunday evening. His chapel is well filled by not a very high style of audience ; however, he will repay your going."

" I went on Monday to the Roman Catholic Cathedral, Southwark ; they played Mozart's Twelfth Mass splendidly, worth all the trouble to hear that. Dr. Boyle (a great authority) told us we might dance and enjoy ourselves till midnight if only we were good Christians and subscribed to the collection—most utter bosh."

" I want to know how you got on with skating. I improved so much those few days that I only had one tumble on the first day of the thaw."

" Have you ever heard Bellew read : he is worth hearing for once : he is a nice-looking man and has a beautiful voice. He read ' The Bridge of Sighs,' Macaulay's ' Naseby ' and Schiller's ' Battle ' with some comic things, and also the last part of ' Enoch Arden.' It was the first thing I had ever heard of the kind, and, as you may imagine, I was exceedingly edified."

" I had a never-to-be-forgotten treat in hearing Mrs. Kemble read ' King Henry VIII '—one of the most wonderful things I ever saw or heard. Catherine pleading in tears—bluff King Harry—Wolsey in his pride, cunning, hypocrisy, and fall : his last address truly magnificent, ending with Catherine's death : you could almost see her die. I heard it remarked that it was overacted : query if that is possible ? If you had heard it we should not soon have heard the end of it. By the by, Baldwin Brown is giving some good lectures on monks and the monkish system : well worth hearing. I am very interested in those old fellows."

" Last Thursday some of us went to hear Gladstone at St. James' Hall speak for ' The Society for the Propagation of the Gospel.' I was a little disappointed, though we ought not to have expected much from so great a man at such a High Church and comparatively small meeting."

" Now, my dear fellow, if you go on in this plaintive strain, lamenting over the mysteries of sin and sorrow that surround us on every side, and pitifully mourning over the want of truth and the fickleness of women, you will come at last to monasticism, and will shut the world out, and seek to hide yourself from its mysteries by the four walls of a hermitage. Is it not a better and nobler thing to rise to the emergency, to brave yourself to stern conflict with what is wrong, and to earnest endeavour to maintain and further the right ? It is no use stopping to moralise over the broken pitcher, or to shed sentimental tears : rather seek to put together the broken fragments."

" For friendship's sake I do not like to conceal from you, or in fact from any one else, the decision to which I have come. So to be frank, I have decided my future course, and am going, with help from above, to be a minister of the Gospel. Now I can imagine your astonishment, but it is a fact. I need only add that it appears to me to be the noblest aim in life to live entirely devoted to the one great object of bringing others to know Him who has accomplished so much for us. When weighed against the hereafter, earth and its careers sink into insignificance."

Of his college career the Rev. John Whitaker, a fellow student, gives some reminiscences, speaking of him as the youngest student whose room had a window overlooking one of the loveliest bits of Regent's Park.

" Tall, slim, fair-looking, he had far more the appearance

B

of a bright boy in the early teens than of a young man on
the verge of twenty. Had he dressed himself in a gown and
parted his hair in the middle, and taken the rôle of a pretty
girl in a charade, the representation would have been
perfect. His ' Tam-o'-shanter ' headpiece and round jacket
gave him a very boyish appearance. All his movements
overflowed with animal spirits, he was full of fun, and ever
alert and active. He was the ' pet ' in the family of students,
admired without envy, and regarded with the deepest
affection by all.

" He had a big heart even then. He was most considerate
and kind. He could not refrain from smiles or restrain loud
laughter at certain mistakes and oddities, but never was
there a sting or a hurt in either speech or act ; his whole
influence was both refining and elevating. Instinctively he
discerned the ' hardships ' of his less fortunate brother, and
was most successful in imparting relief, and inspiring with
hope.

" After the three months' probation the committee set
the door wide open for him on to the full college term of
four years. If in anything he was envied, it was in his
fluent tongue, in his ready pen, in his soaring imagination,
in the ease with which he got through class-work, in his
suggestive questioning or in his ability to debate a point.
The delights of the Common Hall were his speeches—pithy
and spicy—on all sorts of subjects. He was without a rival.
When the rest of his class-mates were ill-prepared, their
prevention of discomfiture was to get him to start a question
which occupied the Principal for the rest of the hour in
answering. When any discontent arose, and a deputation
was appointed to make complaint about the butter or the
cheese, he was always the most successful pleader. When
any leading function had to be discharged on special or
annual occasions, and when numerous guests were present,
we were all quite satisfied with our eloquent representative.
Every week-end some important Church demanded his
services. His gifts were recognised outside as well as inside
the College. His spirit was devout, and when he took the

prayers in his turn it was always a most real and refreshing service.

" We often talked about him behind his back. ' He is a nice fellow ; he has splendid gifts ; there is any amount of go in him ; he will be sure to rise to a top place in the Denomination,' were among the remarks made concerning him. In 1866 we saw the bright spring promise ; now we see the large crop of ripe mellow fruit."

Another glimpse of the College life is given by Mr. Herbert Smith, who was also his fellow-student and became his fast friend, his " chum " in fact. " I remember," he says " how his feelings were stirred by the great ice accident at Regent's Park, when over forty persons were drowned. We were not present at the crash, but were by the shore of the lake a few minutes afterwards when rescues were still being effected. Five of our men were immersed but mercifully escaped. On the following day we all gathered together for a service of thanksgiving and rededication.

" We read Botany together from an ancient book one of us possessed, we also sought to improve ourselves in ' raising the tune.' This we did by betaking ourselves to the top floor of the house, where Meyer's bedroom at that time was situated—remote from all our day-time haunts. After evening prayers, when all the other men trooped into the Common Hall for supper, we got as far apart as we could from each other in the corners of the room, and each with a Bristol Tune Book in our hand, we tried one or two hymns to various tunes. When we wanted a common metre we always burst forth with ' When I can read my title clear, To mansions in the skies.' "

The two students were so inseparable that they became known as " The Siamese Twins." After the day's work Meyer would come into Smith's room and they would read together from Tennyson, Keats, Shelley or Pollock, and on occasion would naturally kneel together in prayer. Quite an ideal fellowship which continued silently all through life. As late as January 28th, 1929, Meyer wrote, " I am

constrained to call you my dear Herbert. How wonderful
that we are both alive and could take up the threads where
we laid them down."

In those early days these two joined in a series of services
in a little building long since demolished—James Street
Chapel, Old Street, St. Luke's, where Mr. E. J. Farley, a
furniture dealer, was Pastor. Their advent was marked by
a tea-meeting on January 1st, 1868, which 107 persons
attended. The tea was provided at fourpence each, and the
young preachers made a profit of one shilling and eightpence.
When they held their next tea-meeting their tender
consciences made them reduce the price to threepence, and
with 112 present they made a loss of five and elevenpence
halfpenny. I write this with the accounts before me.

The hour's tramp from the College and back again
during those five months gave the preachers an appetite, and
on their return they pillaged the larder and carried the
crusts to Meyer's study, and Herbert Smith adds, " If we
had any mending to do, that was the time to do it : so we
munched and sewed on buttons."

Of Dr. Angus, the Principal, who had been Spurgeon's
predecessor and afterwards for a little while Secretary of the
Baptist Missionary Society, he formed a high estimate.
" Dr. Angus I like more and more," he wrote, " both as a
man, a friend, and a teacher." So passed the seemingly
uneventful years of preparation until he reached his majority.
He took his B.A. London University on December 1st, 1869.
The honorary degree of Doctor of Divinity was conferred
upon him in 1911 by MacMaster University, Canada.

His career subsequent to his ordination may be divided
into three epochs. The first including his connection with
the Churches in Richmond, Liverpool and York. The
second his work in Leicester, where he has left his most
enduring monument. The third his fourfold ministry in the
two London Churches of which he was minister. Woven
into the texture of the final section, his world-wide missions
claimed a place and all the while there flowed from his pen

a continuous stream of letters, pamphlets, books and articles, incessant and compelling, so "still the wonder grew, that one small head should carry all he knew." Even on his death-bed, in full view of his departure he dictated answers to his correspondents and letters to his friends ; and who that knew him could doubt but that he passed over to still fuller activity and service on the other side ?

Blessed are they that have their blessed dead.

CHAPTER TWO

The Making of the Minister

LIVERPOOL AND YORK

THE minister in the making devoted himself to the making of a Church. In after years he frequently said that he could not understand the position of a minister out of a job, for if no church called him, he would go out into the open and preach to the people in the streets and find a church for himself ; a thing he actually did at one stage of his career, as we shall see afterwards.

During the second half of his College course he was appointed to the charge of a little group of Baptists in Richmond, and is still gratefully remembered by several aged members of the Church which now worships in Duke Street Chapel, a substantial stone building. The first invitation, still preserved, is dated June 17th, 1868, and his ministry began on July 26th. By arrangement with Dr. Angus the student was to receive twelve shillings a week. On November 14th Mr. Meyer replied to a request that he should undertake the pastorate of the Church, " With unfeigned gratitude do I join with you in blessing God for what He has wrought by me, in answer to our united prayers. To Him and to Him alone be all the glory. . . Believing that this thing is of God, and that He never gives His servants a work to do without also giving them all needed help, in reliance on Him I accept your invitation." Then he states some conditions which do not concern us, asks that the present engagement be only temporary, terminating on the last Sabbath of May 1869, and adds,

" I think that £1 a Sabbath had better be substituted for the £50 per annum."

A letter dated January 20th, 1869, which he addressed to Mr. Spurgeon, who that year was President of the London Baptist Association, set out that the Baptist denomination was most inadequately represented in Richmond, and asked him to help them to establish something more permanent and suitable than the Hall in which the Church worshipped. " And with Christian courtesy and much esteem," he said,

" I remain,
" Yours sincerely,
" F. BROTHERTON MEYER."

So he began.

On a later visit, Mr. Meyer declared that it was one of the old deacons of the Church that had taught him how to preach. This was his first bit of pastoral oversight, and probably he reaped as much benefit from it as the people. It is an excellent thing for a student to study men as well as books, to put into practice the theories learnt in his classes, to balance his theology with search for the souls of the people. That he did this effectively is evidenced by the call they gave him before the end of his College course, to stay with them and establish what they believed would become an influential centre of light in the neighbourhood. But he declared that he was only able to attract humble folk and children, and urged them to look elsewhere for a worthy leader.

Refusing a call to Portland Chapel, Southampton, where Dr. Alexander Maclaren of Manchester started his ministry, he accepted the invitation to become assistant to the Rev. C. M. Birrell at Pembroke Chapel, Liverpool, and began there on January 1st, 1870, the fateful year in the Church of Christ, when the Pope was declared to be infallible.

Letters from Mr. Birrell, still extant, reflect the satisfaction with which the Assistant Minister was welcomed. Under date December 18th, 1869, to Mr. Meyer, he said, " Dr. Angus wrote presenting the difficulty of your unfinished course. I have answered that the case is different from that of a settlement in the sole charge of a town congregation, which might well be expected to put a sudden stop to study by an overwhelming demand for perpetual sermons and public work outside the congregation. Your work in Liverpool would seldom require more than one sermon a week, and time might be arranged for unbroken spaces of study. I should feel it a duty to protect you as much as possible from unnecessary distractions, and make your six months really a continuation of your Collegiate course."

Five days later in another letter he writes: " Just a word to say how glad I have been to receive your acceptance of our proposal. All the future is wisely concealed from us, yet I think we have the fullest warrant for trusting that this important step has been taken under divine direction, and that we may look for a great blessing in it. It was only constitutional for the President of the College to demur ; and right for me, the aggressor, to make the most liberal concession. *The conclusion was none the less inevitable.* We shall look for you on New Year's Day."

There are other letters showing the cordial relation which subsisted between the two. When his Assistant was preaching in some other place, he wrote, " You may try your last sermon here over again for the evening. It had, as most of your sermons have, the main things, and was compact, and easily understood." An interesting sidelight on his early style.

An invitation to strengthen the bond between the two was passed by the Church on May 23rd, 1870. " That the Reverend Frederick Brotherton Meyer, B.A., be respectfully and affectionately invited to be the Associate of the Pastor of this Church in all public and private services of the ministry." This arrangement, with a salary of £200 a year, came into operation on July 1st, 1870.

Baldwin Brown wrote his congratulations to Mr. Meyer on his connection with Mr. Birrell. " There is no man in England more entirely and cordially respected, and I know

no one with whom a young minister like yourself would be
more likely to co-operate happily, and to his own advantage
and culture both as a preacher and pastor. For no doubt
you feel that your real education is just beginning now.
Never till we get out into life do we feel the full pressure
which the Great Master puts on the pupils in His High
School."

All that is emphasised by Mr. Meyer himself. " To have
known Mr. Birrell," he writes in *The Bells of Is*, " is to have
known one of the sweetest, holiest, most catholic, and most
cultured men of his time. He was richly endowed by
nature in his erect and elegant figure, his intellectual face,
with its flashing expressive eye and noble expanse of fore-
head surmounted by the abundance of raven hair. His
preaching was deeply spiritual, full of cultured thought,
expressed in polished and classic phrase. But it was in his
conversational powers that he was *facile princeps*. It was
a rich treat to sit with him in the evening after supper, and
let him talk of men he had known, of places he had visited,
books he had read, and ceremonials he had witnessed.
Oh ! rare and glorious man, will it ever be my lot again to
be admitted into thy inner fellowship ! Surely thou wilt
be too much sought after in that world where such as thou
art take the first rank amongst their peers."

This, of course, is the rhapsody of a hero worshipper,
and reflects the impressions of a young and ardent soul.
Quite probably the receptivity of the young assistant called
forth the old minister's powers—there are good listeners as
well as good talkers. In the charming family circle was
numbered the son, Augustine Birrell, then a student three
years younger than Meyer, since so well known as author
and statesman.

F. B. Meyer soon became Birrellised ; sometimes of set
purpose, and more often unconsciously taking the colour
and imitating the methods and mannerisms of his master.
Birrell's plan of sermonising was something like Dr. Jowett's
in later years. Every sentence was polished and balanced.
Then the written discourse was committed to memory and

recited in the pulpit. This is the most laborious and least satisfactory form of preaching ; the very perfection of the phrasing is apt to come between the soul of the preacher and the soul of the hearer, the mind of the preacher is fixed on the words rather than on the people, the appeal is from intellect to intellect rather than from heart to heart. But it has its attraction to those who know anything of the witchery of words, and the younger man followed the older, gaining indeed concentration and style in the process, but getting into bondage from which afterwards he was only delivered by a great spiritual crisis. But here, as elsewhere, the law was the schoolmaster to bring him to Christ. He declared himself that he had destroyed uncounted reams of paper in writing and correcting and revising his productions in those early years ; probably the discipline conduced even more to his readiness of utterance in the later years.

Sermon-making was not the only discipline of this time. The position of an Assistant Minister is never very easy, however considerate his senior may be. He is apt to be overlooked in important occasions, and scarcely welcomed as a substitute in the lesser events of the Church. But the young minister, unable to compete in the pulpit as yet, speedily found a place in pastoral visitation. Here his Richmond experience served him in good stead, and he soon became welcome in the homes of the people for his courteous and tactful ways. And for thirty months he greatly contributed to the wealth of the church-life.

On February 20th, 1871, scarcely more than a year after his settlement in Liverpool, his marriage, two months before his twenty-fourth birthday, to Miss J. E. Jones, of Birkenhead, was celebrated. He came, he saw, and was conquered by this lady of fascinating personality, creative imagination, and undeviating will. With the impetuosity of youth and the independence of manhood, once he had determined his course, he brooked no delay in the fulfilment of his purpose, and for more than fifty-eight years he rendered to Mrs. Meyer most chivalrous devotion.

A special meeting of the Church on January 16th, 1872,

passed a resolution saying, " That it could not receive the communication of the Rev. F. B. Meyer, intimating that his cordial co-operation with our pastor is so soon to terminate, without conveying to him the assurance of its grateful appreciation of his faithful and unrelaxing efforts to promote its spiritual welfare, and of his earnest endeavours for the salvation of the unconverted in the congregation and neighbourhood. It will be the sincere prayer of the church," says the resolution, which was signed by the Pastor and ten deacons, " that he may be guided to such a sphere of usefulness as shall be conducive to the happiness of himself and Mrs. Meyer, and that they may long rejoice together in the manifestations of Divine blessing attending their service for our Lord and Master."

The wish for guidance was fulfilled when, on March 19th, 1872, a special gathering of the Church in York " earnestly, anxiously, and unanimously begged his acceptance of an invitation to become its pastor ; prayerfully hoping that he would see the finger of the Almighty pointing him to York." This was forwarded to him on April 3rd, signed by sixty-three members of the Church. The invitation was accepted, Mr. and Mrs. Meyer with their infant daughter moved to their new home, and the first sermon of the new ministry was preached on the first Sunday in May.

On the eve of his departure from Liverpool, at a meeting of Farewell, a purse of sixty guineas and eight volumes of Kitto's Biblical Illustrations were presented to Mr. Meyer, to which Mr. Birrell added a handsomely bound volume on *The Christian Ministry*, in commemoration of many conferences they had had on that subject.

Mr. and Mrs. Meyer had one daughter and three grandchildren—two grand-daughters and also one grandson, to whom his grandparents were greatly attached, until in the War he gave his life for his country at Vimy Ridge. In her husband's earlier journeyings abroad, Mrs. Meyer sometimes accompanied him, though owing to indifferent health, she never took much share in his work of ministry. Their home life, begun in Liverpool, was continued at York and at Leicester, until in the latter city, in order that Mrs. Meyer might spend the winter in Cannes with her daughter, the home was broken up and Mr. Meyer went into rooms. Afterwards, in London, they made their home first at Hampstead and then in Portman Mansions for more than thirty years, and so it continued until the end.

In death they were scarcely divided. Mrs. Meyer found it necessary to go into a Nursing Home in Bournemouth for treatment ; quite unexpectedly after a fortnight she became unconscious, and Dr. Meyer hastened to her side and remained with her until she died. It was from the same Home, two months later, that he himself passed over.

On March 17th, 1929, he wrote to the Rev. M. E. Aubrey, Secretary of the Baptist Union, some characteristic words, " Will you kindly thank the Council of the Baptist Union for their most kind and valued sympathy in the Home-Call of my wife. Though this gap in the home, after so many years of married life, is always crying out, it is good to know that those least able to bear the strain of life are for ever shielded."

So the minister was made.

CHAPTER THREE

MOODY AND MEYER

THE two formative years in Liverpool were followed by two critical years in York. York Minster, one of the finest church buildings in the world, vies with Amiens Cathedral in grandeur and suggestiveness ; its windows are over-whelming in their beauty, and its history as one of the earliest scenes of Christian worship in the country renders it unique. The Baptist Chapel in Priory Street, which in itself is an artistic building, is dwarfed by the magnificence of the Minster, but perhaps the early saints if they returned to earth might find themselves more at home in the humbler than in the mightier shrine.

The city has had the experience of one of the greatest preachers, merely considered as a preacher, that England has ever known. On Mr. Meyer's advent the glamour of the ministry of " James Parsons of York " was still over the people. Paxton Hood speaks of him as " the most impressive orator we have ever known." Because Meyer was himself destined to approach him in style and influence, the following extract from *The Throne of Eloquence* may be applied to both preachers.

" Listening to him the irresistible force of an exceedingly quiet power crept over one, through one ; we felt the words tingling along the blood ; it was as if dim spectral forms hovered before the eyes, *and still the magnetic stream runs on*. You suspend your breath in fixed feeling : not a word must be lost, for that might be *the* word : you are passive before the magnetist : your eye dilated to catch the vision rising before the spirit : you feel that the preacher's eye is on you : it fascinates you : you cannot release yourself from it, you would not if you could, *and still the magnetic stream runs on.* You surrender yourself to the dominion of your master ; he clasps you in the slumber of genius, and now you are clairvoyant. It is the day of final judgment ! You see, or seem to see, a million snaky fires piercing through the windows of the old church : fold above fold they coil in spiral press : the roof of the temple is rent : the whole infinite is stretched before you : each word from the preacher adds something to the terror of the impression, *for still the magnetic stream runs on.* You are wrapped in a painful sense of conscious unconsciousness, from which you are roused, to your boundless gratitude and joy, by the ceasing of the flow of the magnetic stream. Two or three thousand people are unanimously coughing to confirm you in the half-belief that you are still on earth, and in the pulpit before you, apparently ignorant that he has said anything remarkable, the preacher is collecting his electricity for another attack upon some other soul."

Paxton Hood then goes on to describe the preaching as sometimes resembling a rippling stream, but always there was the same quiet power and abiding influence. Those who knew F. B. Meyer can make the comparison for themselves.

In the summer of their first year in York, the little family paid a pleasant visit to Grandmamma Sturt at Clapham, and writing to his aunt at Pembury she said, " The Church at York is progressing from every point of view. Our young Timothy is altogether worthy, living by faith and looking upward, striving to do his work." With the style he had acquired in contact with Mr. Birrell, and his experience of pastoral work, he made a decided appeal to the new congregation, especially to the young men, who gathered round him even from beyond the boundaries of his own church. But there was only a scanty record of conversions, and though he became popular he scarcely imagined himself to be successful as a minister of Jesus Christ.

Then came the experience which affected his whole after-life and made his years in York ever memorable.

D. L. Moody and Ira D. Sankey had crossed the Atlantic and landed in Liverpool, only to find to their dismay that the two men who had invited them to England, Rev. W. Pennefather of Barnet, and Mr. Cuthbert Bainbridge of Newcastle, had both recently died.   Scarcely knowing where to turn, Moody remembered that in Western America some time before, a visitor had told him that if he ever came to England, he would be glad to see him, and urged him not to forget two words, " Bennett, York." Mr. Bennett was a chemist in the city, a little man whom I subsequently came to know quite well ; he conducted a Mission Hall in a needy district with considerable success.   Knowing nothing beyond the fact that he had once suggested a visit to York, the evangelists telegraphed to Bennett : " Self, wife and children, Sankey and wife just arrived, shall we come on." He burst into Meyer's study with the message and they replied " Come on."   So without preliminary announcement they arrived, and on the Sunday they conducted services in the city.   On Monday a noon prayer meeting had been convened in a little room in Coney Street and the local ministers had been invited.   Meyer was amongst those who attended, and in spite of the differences between Moody and himself, he felt drawn to the stranger. He recognised beneath his rugged utterance a spiritual power which he himself longed to possess, and straightway a series of meetings to extend over ten days was arranged to be held in Salem Congregational Church, James Parsons' Church, of which Dr. John Hunter was then the minister. Afterwards the meetings were held in Priory Street Church, and the Minister's Vestry there will always be sacred as the place where the fire that lighted England during the succeeding years began to burn.   There, day after day, in the mornings, a little group gathered for prayer, and afterwards in the church there were some memorable meetings.

That was the beginning of a life-long devotion between the two men. Moody never forgot that Meyer was the first minister heartily to welcome him to England, and Meyer never forgot that he learnt from Moody the art of winning

men and women for Christ. In visiting the Bible Institute
in Chicago two years ago, I at once noticed that in the office
there were but two large photographs on the wall—
D. L. Moody and F. B. Meyer ; Meyer as I first came to
know him in 1884, with a round, sunny face, a suspicion of
whiskers on each side of it, and clear eyes looking hopefully
out on the world. In an inner room I discovered a quaint
picture of Moody, in a peaked cap, gathering the scholars
for his first Sunday School class.

Perhaps the chief lesson Moody taught the young
pastor was that to do good work in the world he must be
himself, not becoming a mere copy of somebody else, and by
contact with the man whom Henry Drummond described as
" the greatest human he ever met " he was lifted from
merely parochial or denominational ideas of Christ's work
in the world. In fact Meyer became an evangelist himself—
no small result of the York Mission.

Two or three years ago I asked a number of successful
preachers " What in your judgment is the secret of pulpit
power ? " Instead of a direct answer Dr. George Morrison
of Glasgow gave me an incident. " John Kelman told me
this summer a very interesting story. When he was
colleague to Dr. Whyte he became alarmed lest people might
think there was too great a discrepancy between his preaching
and that of Dr. Whyte. He accordingly prepared and
preached a sermon along Whyte's own lines. It was
Dr. Whyte's custom in the vestry afterwards always to
thank Dr. Kelman. This day he did not thank him, but,
after walking once or twice up and down the vestry, he laid
his hand on Kelman's shoulder and said to him very
earnestly, ' John, preach your own message.' " The
answers from the other preachers are very illuminating, but
this is to the point here. Meyer began to preach his own
message. Began. For swinging off from Birrell he became
tinctured with Moody, and another lesson yet awaited his
learning.

He does not seem to have been greatly impressed with
Mr. Sankey, though Moody owed more to his singing

companion in subsequent days than can be estimated. The innovation of the American organ and solo singing in a service seemed to some people irreverent. Philip Phillips had preceded him from America and aroused much interest in this country, but he only gave recitals, and that word covered the novelty. Something else was needed to commend the new method in a mission. At length the evangelists hit upon a formula that disarmed all criticism. " Mr. Moody will preach and Mr. Sankey will sing the Gospel." With my own experience for fifteen years alongside my colleague, Manton Smith, I can only bless God for both singers.

But years afterwards when Meyer prepared some notes for the Simultaneous Mission in London, after reference to the various classes with whom the missioners would then have to deal he gave as his considered judgment " *You will have to do with the choir*. This will, in some cases, be the most delicate duty of all. It is certain that solo and anthem singing may become a great snare to spiritual worship unless the choir leader and organist are distinctly spiritual people. But conciliation and tact will stand you in good stead. Only it must be understood that during the Mission the singing must be subordinated to the spiritual results you are desiring. It is not often that a solo or anthem helps a mission service. I am not sure that the ordinary solo or anthem helps any service."

Once in Canada prior to a meeting he was heard to pray, " Help me to be patient while the choir sings, and let them not distract the people from the message we want them to get."

When the evangelists had finished their five weeks' work in York they moved on to Darlington, and a letter written in large script, evidently by Mr. Sankey, dated October 23rd, 1873, is in my left hand as I write. " Dear Brother Meyer, can't you stop off one train as you go through this place. We would like to see you again. A good work here. Drop us a line and we will meet you if we can.

" Yours, working for *Him*,

" Moody and Sankey."

This was not the first visit that Mr. Moody had paid to England. Dr. Campbell Morgan, in his book, *The Practice of Prayer*, tells of his previous visit and of the secret that lay behind it. His references, of course, refer to the year the book was published.

" There are saints of God who for long, long years have been shut off from all the activities of the Church, and even from the worship of the Sanctuary ; but who, nevertheless, have continued to labour together in prayer with the whole fellowship of the saints. There comes to me the thought of one woman, who to my knowledge since 1872 in this great babel of London has been in perpetual pain, and yet in constant prayer. She is to-day a woman twisted and distorted by suffering, and yet exhaling the calm and strength of the secret of the Most High.

" In 1872 she was a bedridden girl in the north of London, praying that God would send Revival to the Church of which she was a member, and yet into which even then she never came. She had read in the little paper called *Revival*, which subsequently became *The Christian*, the story of a work being done in Chicago among ragged children by a man called Moody, but putting that little paper under her pillow, she began to pray : ' O Lord, send this man to our Church.'

" She had no means of reaching him or communicating with him. He had already visited the country in 1867, and in 1872 he started again for a short trip without any intention of doing any work. Mr. Lessey, however, the pastor of the Church of which this girl was a member, met him and asked him to preach for him. He consented, and after the evening service he asked those who would decide for Christ to rise, and hundreds did so. He was surprised, and imagined that his request had been misunderstood. He repeated it more clearly, and again the response was the same. Meetings were continued throughout the following ten days, and four hundred members were taken into the Church. In telling me this story Moody said, ' I wanted to know what this meant. I began making enquiries, and never rested until

I found a bedridden girl praying that God would bring me to that Church. He had heard her, and brought me over four thousand miles of land and sea in answer to her request.'

" This story is told in the *Life of D. L. Moody* by his son : but now let me continue it. That girl was a member of my Church when I was pastor at New Court [London]. She is still a member, still suffering, still confined to her room. When in 1901 I was leaving England for America I went to see her. She said to me, ' I want you to reach that birthday book.' I did so and turning to February 5th, I saw in the handwriting I knew so well : *D. L. Moody, Psa. xci.* Then Marianne Adlard said to me, ' He wrote that for me when he came to see me in 1872, and I prayed for him every day till he went Home to God.' Continuing, she said, ' Now will you write your name on your birthday page and let me pray for you until either you or I go Home.' I shall never forget writing my name in that book. To me the room was full of the Presence. I have often thought of that hour in the rush of busy life, in the place of toil and strain, and even yet, by God's good grace, I know that Marianne Adlard is praying for me ; and it is for this reason that to her in sincere love and admiration I have dedicated this book."

It was on one of these previous visits that Mr. Moody attended " The Believers' Conference " at Dublin, and, walking in Mr. Bewley's garden Henry Varley said in his hearing, " The world has yet to see what God can do with a thoroughly consecrated man." Instantly Moody's heart responded, " God helping me, I will be that man." He went back to America, and realising the need of something to attract the people in order that he might preach to them, found Sankey, persuaded him to join forces, and so they came. Seemingly cut off from all human help on their arrival, but thrown back on God, they gloriously survived.

T. H. Darlow in writing of Miss Havergal's experience on Advent Sunday, December 2nd, 1873, when she first saw clearly the blessedness of true consecration, says, " We may trace some outward signs and tokens of the widespread quickening which visited Great Britain between

1870 and 1876, and was felt, for the time being, almost like a change of religious climate. Water from hidden fountains rose silently in ancient wells of drought. Even so cautious and thoughtful an observer as Hort, writing to Westcott in the first week of 1873, described an impressive devotional service in the University Church of Cambridge, and added, " Assuredly the springs of life are strangely breaking forth anew."

God had His chosen men for the new era. Moody and Meyer were two of them, and, to quote again, " There is no argument which arrests common men like the argument from the aureole."

In later years these two men were destined to be associated also on the other side of the Atlantic. Mr. Meyer was for years one of the popular speakers at the Northfield Conventions originated by Mr. Moody.

" Northfield," he wrote, " is always beautiful, and doubly so after the hot five hours' journey from New York. A single line runs from Springfield to South Vernon, along the valley to which the Connecticut River gives its name. Ten minutes' sharp climb brings us to the village of Northfield, with its one long main road, shaded on either side by a continuous line of noble elms. And there is the view, always beautiful, stretching up the valley to the north-west, with the river gleaming below, to the undulating hills on either side : whilst far away in the distance is a range of mountains—the highest in New England.

" In the main road Mr. Moody meets us. His buggy and horse are known everywhere. At all hours, from early dawn, you are liable to meet him. ' Meet me at the New Auditorium ' is the word of command. So, hastily depositing our baggage at the door of the annexe of the hotel, we make straight tracks for this more recent addition to the noble buildings which are arising at Mr. Moody's end of Northfield.

" It was an amazing sight to see the Auditorium that morning. From an area of twenty miles round the country poured in its contributions, in every reasonable kind of vehicle, and all the roads and the fields were filled with the tethered horses standing contentedly in their slight harness. It seemed as if a crown had been put upon Mr. Moody's life, that here, amid those who have known him from his boyhood, he should be honoured, respected, and beloved, as not even in the greatest missions he had ever held. And during his sermon he was not ashamed to point out his old employer, for whom he used to work when he was a lad."

Moody used sometimes to tell of Meyer's introduction to the assembly at Northfield. With charming naïveté and childlike egotism his first sentence was, "You must not expect the blessing because I have come to you." In that sentence his simplicity and masterfulness are revealed. Nobody but he would have said it, and anybody but he would have at once seen its implication; but he went sublimely and unconsciously on and made a deep impression. He was quite sure of himself because he had committed his way unto the Lord.

Another incident which in the memorial notices is going the round of the American papers, is almost as revealing. After some years Dr. Campbell Morgan appeared at Northfield and commanded large audiences. To more than one person Meyer opened his heart as he walked over the grounds, confessing that he found himself liable to be jealous. He said that at first he gave popular addresses and had great crowds, but afterwards his devotional talks were more sparsely attended, while the crowds thronged to Campbell Morgan's Bible Studies. "The only way I can conquer my feeling," Meyer is reported to have said, "is to pray for him daily, which I do." There is in that a certain scrupulosity which sometimes surprised even those who loved him most. Probably what he condemned in himself as jealousy was but a passing mental comparison, and if his sensitive soul had not been centred on himself the thought would have passed like a breath on a mirror. The writers who record this incident and praise him for what they term his humility should rather have brushed the incident aside as the foible of a heart delicately poised.

Another glimpse of the two great souls is supplied by

Mrs. Banks, in whose home Mr. Meyer always had hospitality during the Keswick Convention. One year Mr. Moody was detained in England owing to the illness of his son, and he took the opportunity of visiting the Keswick Convention. Mr. Meyer agreed to go to Northfield for him if he would take the service of the Congregational Church at Keswick. The night before he sailed the two met with a few friends at Mrs. Banks's house. " Never can I forget," she says, " these two saintly men praying one for the other. It was a wonderful time of communion." As it was impossible to accommodate in the little church those who wished to hear Mr. Moody, the Tent was placed at the disposal of the Church by the Trustees of the Convention, and of course there was an overwhelming service. Mr. Moody also spoke at the Testimony Meeting, and with tears streaming down his cheeks gave as his experience, " Son, I am with thee for ever, and all that I have is thine."

The following letters, written in his large script, widely spaced, will be of interest, showing something of Moody's methods and his confidence in Meyer :—

" *March 14th* (no year).

" MY DEAR MEYER,

" Cable me that you will give Northfield the month of August and I will work night and day to get ministers there for all the month, and if you could lay out a course and let me advertise it we will give you ministers from all over the land. This country needs it far more than I can tell you, and I do hope you will come. I think you can do more with us in a month that you can in London in a year. But we should know at once if you will come. You need not give but one lecture a day, and I think we can keep the town full all the month if you let us know now if you can come. ' Moody, Northfield, Mass. Will come ' is all you need to send. You need not sign your name. And I will set all the wheels in motion to bring all to Northfield that we can—do come and let it be settled at once, so we can go ahead. This country is ready for your teaching as never before, and you can touch every part of it if you will come.

" Yours as ever,
" D. L. MOODY."

On March 31st, 1894, he wrote :—

" I want you for all of August, only one lecture a day. I am putting up a new building that will accommodate 2,500, and I want you to be the man to teach in it for thirty days, and I will go to work and get the ministers there. My plan is to get them there by the hundreds. I think I will keep up the Convention for about fifteen days, and then have you go on for fifteen days more, and if we begin now we can keep the meetings full all the month. Now do not decline to come."

" February 16th, 1897.

" MY DEAR MEYER,

" My dear Brother, let me tell you how glad I am that you came to this country. I find it is much easier to preach in Boston and New York than it was last month. The ministers have got a great blessing, and I am hearing all about that they preached different last Sabbath. I trust the Good Lord will take you safely back to your own land, and soon bring you back to this country. It will never be known in time what amount of good you have done in fourteen days you have been with us, and hundreds of thousands will follow you across the deep with their prayer.

" I hope you will let me know the first day you can be with us again, and stay as long as you can and help us in this great country, for our need is great.

" Your true friend,
" D. L. MOODY."

Under date February 23rd, 1897, he wrote :—

" I do not think you will ever know on earth what you did or what the Lord did through you. I am hearing all the time of blessing."

On March 8th, 1897, Mr. Meyer himself gave an account of his visit, and that may fitly finish this chapter.

" The fortnight I spent in America was certainly the most wonderful time of my life ; and into it was crowded a lifetime. If I had lived for nothing else in the world—lived, and studied, and suffered for nothing else than to spend that fortnight in America—I should have lived to good purpose.

" It was prepared for by a good deal of failure, dissatisfaction, and consciousness of need. For many years the pulpit in America has been too much given over to sensational preaching. Instead of what we should call textual, expository preaching, the great preachers have sought rather to develop topics, and they have therefore given themselves up to the treatment of subjects of burning interest, either in the political or social world.

" Then there has been a growing worldliness on the part of the churches. Fairs, social parties for raising the minister's stipend, the introduction into the house of God of elements which we should taboo as being altogether unworthy, have been in vogue.

" Not only has there been a tendency in the direction of sensationalism and worldliness, but also of a spurious revivalism ; that is to say, when the numerical increase has been unsatisfactory, and when the life of God in the churches has been diminishing, instead of going back to God Himself and to His Word and prayer to revive the churches, there has been too large a disposition to call in revivalistic preachers, and to use every method in the newspapers by advertising, and in every way to get up a revival, the reaction from which has been disastrous. These influences have been preparing the way for a great yearning on the part of ministers and people for a deeper and richer and more Scriptural life.

" There has been another influence which I must refer to for a moment. In that wonderful new land there is a great freedom given to all new methods, and to new conceptions of Scripture. And these have grown up like mushrooms, and have prejudiced the minds of thinking people, especially ministers, against what is known as *the movement for the Deepening of the Spiritual Life*. I was told by one man, who knew America well, that if I went to America I must never mention a word about holiness if I desired to make people really holy. There has been so much prejudice raised by certain schools of teaching, which have had great power in America, that there has been a revulsion from the special teaching which some of us love and preach. So that was another element of considerable difficulty.

" In the meanwhile Mr. Moody has been for some years gathering at Northfield a conference—not unlike our Mildmay Conference—for the promulgation of Scriptural truth and the great evangelical doctrines. That conference till within ten years ago devoted itself almost exclusively to the exposition of the Word of God. Then Mr. Moody asked some of us to visit Northfield. I had the pleasure of going there for four successive summer conferences, and came into close accord with my beloved friend, now gone, Dr. Gordon. Dr. Gordon became the representative in that country of the movement for the Deepening of the Spiritual Life, and he with others of us began to teach at Northfield the necessity for entire consecration, faith in the keeping power of God, and the necessity of receiving the enduement of the Holy Spirit of Pentecost.

" This last doctrine especially was caught up with great avidity, and from this Conference ministers, who had attended in large numbers, went to all parts of the States as those who had themselves passed through a baptism of fire. And Mr. Moody heard, as we heard, that in all parts of America there was a great crying out for the enduement of the Holy Ghost. This movement was working away through the States, and was very much stimulated by the visit of Mr. Webb-Peploe and Mr. Andrew Murray the summer before last. Meanwhile my own books had been very largely circulated in the States, and by Mr. Moody's constant introduction of my books, and also by my addresses, my name became familiar with them, and it seemed as if I should act as an exponent of this deeper teaching. He urged me to come, and I said I would come for a fortnight only.

" When I reached Boston on the Thursday night I was at once hurried to an immense meeting of six thousand ' Endeavourers,' and from them to another crowded meeting at

Tremont Temple, of about three thousand people, at which
I made the presentation to Mr. Moody of the £2,600 which
the British Christians had entrusted me with. I knew I
must do it then, because with characteristic modesty,
Mr. Moody was preparing to leave by the night train to
spend his birthday at Northfield, and I knew that if I did
not strike at that very moment I should have missed the
chance. And so, as soon as he had shaken hands with me
and introduced me, I stood up and, in the name of Lord
Kinnaird, Prebendary Webb-Peploe and others, I presented
to him the gift of the British Christians, which very much
touched him and stirred the immense audience to the very
heart. I may say that they have raised on their part
£3,000, so that the chapel at Northfield on which we had
set our hearts is now secure, and will at once be proceeded
with.

" Then he left me and I had three days alone in Boston.
The audiences crowded Tremont Temple. We had to begin
half an hour before the time, and in the morning at half-past
ten the place would be crowded, and again in the afternoon.
All the time, whenever I spoke in Boston in the Tremont
Temple it would be full, or if in any chapel, like Dr. Gordon's,
it would be crowded to suffocation. The people were
standing all around and would stand sometimes for an
hour.

" At the end of my addresses there I met about four
hundred ministers at the invitation of Dr. Lorimer. They
questioned me pretty closely about my teaching. I had
been very careful to show that the Holy Ghost is in us, but
that He was received on us as an anointed power. I was
able to answer all their questions, I think, satisfactorily ;
and at the close of that very memorable meeting, by the
lips of Dr. Lorimer, they accepted what I taught. Then we
knelt together and received from God an overwhelming
baptism of His most blessed Spirit. I believe that meeting
will be the beginning of an era in the life of many of our
beloved brethren in Boston.

" I shall never forget preaching in Dr. Gordon's Church.

It was the second anniversary of his death. The tide of
emotion rose as high as it could.

"I took the midnight train to New York, and found
Mr. Moody more anxious than I have ever seen him. For
months before he had been working up to those meetings.
I hardly realised how much he had staked until I went down
to the Carnegie Rooms, which are like an opera-house, with
tiers of boxes and galleries, and capable of holding about
2,500 people. I found he had arranged ten meetings for me
there—in the morning at half-past ten, and in the afternoon
at half-past three. To my utter bewilderment, every
morning when I went there the place was filled, and
in the afternoon it was crowded in every part. In front
of me there was always a reserved area for five hundred
ministers and I had a great body of divinity sitting
there ! Most sympathetic those men were—brothers
indeed.

"Most marvellously the climate of New York—I found
out afterwards it is quite a common occurrence—seriously
affected my voice. I think I never passed through an agony
in my whole life like it. Very often I could not speak above
a whisper ; I never was in such a case before, yet I was
bound to go through those ten addresses. But every time
I got up from sleep my voice came back to me. I never was
so utterly thrown on Christ. I used to talk just in the
simplest way and to say, ' Lord, it seems madness ' ; but
Dr. Pierson told me that in his judgment that had been one
of the blessed conditions of success, because it so utterly
eliminated me and made Christ so utterly prominent that
people were attracted to Him.

"At the end of these meetings in the Carnegie Rooms
I met the New York ministers, a vast gathering, in one of
their large Presbyterian churches. And again they questioned
me. They asked me to distinguish between dying to self and
the death of self ; whether the enduement of the Holy
Spirit is intermittent or permanent ; and questions of that
sort. Just as soon as my brethren found that the teaching
was consistent with theology, and above all with the Bible,

I received their God-speed, and again we sought the enduement of the Holy Ghost.

" Then I went to Philadelphia, and the next two days
were utterly wonderful. Mr. Chapman had arranged a
meeting of ministers on the Monday morning. I thought
there might be one hundred ministers in attendance, but
when I came into the large Presbyterian Church—one of the
largest in the city—I found it crowded from side to side with
ministers, and all around me on the platform there were
seated venerable servants of Christ. I stood up, leaning
heavily on Christ, for I knew that everything depended on
Him. As I began to talk to that audience I felt I was being
looked at and measured and reckoned up. But all that
passed away within ten minutes, and the whole audience
seemed melted under the power of God. We adjourned to
lunch and then gathered to hear about the enduement of the
Holy Ghost ; then at night a vast meeting. And next day a
meeting at one of their colleges, over which Dr. Weston
presides ; another meeting of ministers, who again questioned
and catechised me ; and at the end a vast meeting at which
three thousand people crowded the place on the Tuesday
night. At this gathering there was the utmost hush, and a
deep sense of the presence of God, and a reception by faith
of the Holy Ghost. And so I passed away.

" But I am certain of this, that in America the interest
for the moment has turned from the conversion of men from
the outside world to the revival of the Church. The other
will come presently. But meanwhile ministers and people
are coming back to God, to Pentecost, to the Holy Ghost ;
and in my judgment this is wanted as much in England as in
that great country. And what I would say to every evangelist and to every Christian worker is, that our great need,
now that this age is coming near to an end, and that every
sign in the world indicates the near break-up of the present
era and the introduction of the new era—what I would say
is that there is nothing more urgently necessary than that
every one of us should get back to the enduement of the
Holy Ghost. I have great faith that God is going to bless

us—I know not when, or how, or where, except that it is along this line of the enduement of the Holy Ghost. The Church has had her former rain and God is about to give her the latter rain also. But it must begin with us. Let us put away our sectarianism ; it is the curse of the Church ! Put away this back-biting, this merciless criticism of one another's methods, this perpetual jealousy—sweep it all away before the tide of the love of God, and then the great world of men will be reached presently."

CHAPTER FOUR

Upheaval and Adventure

THE scene now moves south. From York Mr. Meyer went to Leicester. Leicester, the city which is nearer the centre of England than any other ! Leicester, the site of a Roman Camp as the " cester " in its name implies ! Leicester, where was held the first Parliament of England under Simon de Montfort ! Leicester, where Cardinal Wolsey in dying wished he had served his God with half the zeal he had served his country ! Leicester, where William Carey meditated on the needs of the world and went forth to India ! Leicester, where Robert Hall, the greatest preacher of his day, in spite of unrelieved pain, held his congregations spellbound ! To Leicester came F. B. Meyer, to add another illustrious name to its roll, though his early experiences in the city gave scant promise of such renown.

Victoria Road Church, a commanding structure, stands conspicuous on the rise of the hill on the road to London. As the town was extending, a few public-spirited men, of whom my wife's father was one, had sufficient foresight and enterprise to build the church, and when the tidings of the death of Dr. Nathaniel Haycroft, its first minister, reached Mr. Meyer in York, he had an instant presentiment that he would be his successor. In spite of the encouragement he had received in the northern city it scarcely seemed as if the Church in York was his fitting sphere, and yet there was nothing to suggest to him that the people in Leicester had ever even heard of him. But an invitation to preach there reached him, and on June 4th, 1874, the Church at a special meeting resolved, " That the Deacons be empowered and

requested to send a cordial and earnest invitation to the
Rev. F. B. Meyer, B.A., York, to become the pastor of
this church and congregation, and to make all necessary
arrangements." In passing it may be noted that
Mrs. Fullerton was one of the junior members of the church
who joined in the invitation. In forwarding this resolution,
written on blue paper, the four deacons who signed the
letter, say, " We desire to state that our attention had been
frequently directed to you during the past year, and some of
our friends had heard you preach at York." Then follow
some expressions of desire that, in addition to the ministra-
tions of the pulpit, pastoral visitation should not be
overlooked, and that the church would meet the expenses
of removal and " guarantee an annual salary of four hundred
guineas a year."

In August, 1874, farewell was therefore said to York,
and the ministry in Leicester began with high hopes on the
first Sunday of September. But these hopes were not
destined to be fulfilled. Nearly four years of work, not un-
blessed, were added at Leicester to the four years that had
preceded them, and then came the Upheaval. If he had
gone straight from Liverpool to Leicester he might have
succeeded in meeting the needs of the people there and
attracting an influential congregation, but the amalgam of
Birrell and Moody unfitted him for it. No longer could his
soul, that had been stirred by his contact with the evangelistic ardour of those throbbing weeks in York, be content
only to care for those within the influence of his church
while the crowds surged past its doors. He had learnt from
Moody to be natural, but he had not yet learned to adapt
means to ends, and in applying mission methods he
estranged some of his best helpers, who were not prepared
for such novelties. In later years it became a recognised
thing to ask enquirers to give some indication of their
desire, but in those earlier days things were more decorous
and reserved. The deacons agreed to the establishment of
a mission down-town, but strongly objected to anything
but the accustomed routine at the church : the tension

tightened, and at length Mr. Meyer felt compelled to resign what had appeared to be such a fair prospect of ministerial usefulness, preaching his last sermon at Victoria Road on May 5th, 1878. Of course there was a very decided cleavage of opinion : a large number of the more aggressive members of the congregation were in sympathy with their minister, but those on whom the responsibility of the church chiefly rested were adverse, and since Meyer could not change his methods or moderate his zeal, the best thing was to withdraw.

Writing to Dr. Meyer for his birthday in 1926, Mr. Alfred C. Vick recalls the early Leicester days. " It is a long way back to the old Victoria Road Wednesday Afternoon Children's Service which you used to conduct. It may cheer you to know that one incident at least has been a constant help to me through all the succeeding years. You may have forgotten that week by week you exhibited coloured pictures illustrating the Pilgrim's Progress. You had shown us the picture of the man throwing water on the fire, and asked us, ' Why doesn't the fire go out ? ' Saying you would show us the secret in the next picture you had actually placed your pointer under the top sheet and commenced to throw it over the easel, when you let the pointer drop *before* we had got a glimpse of the picture underneath. You then said, ' No, I'll not show you to-day. Go home and try and think it out for yourselves WHY the fire still burns, and I will show you NEXT WEEK the secret.' Never before or since have I looked forward to seeing a picture with such impatience—it was an interminable week. May I pay my tribute at this late date to that incident, and *its ever-present help during all the years since.* I did not find out the secret till you revealed it the following Wednesday, but, oh ! how often had that Holy Man Christ Jesus poured oil of peace over the little fire burning in me, when the devil (in the shape of circumstances) has been doing his utmost to extinguish the spark."

It seemed as if his work in Leicester was finished. Several churches in the country, hearing of the impending change, approached him to ascertain his willingness to come to them : one—the church at Glossop Road, Sheffield, with a church building somewhat similar to that in Leicester—sent him a definite invitation to the pastorate, and he was so greatly attracted to it that, after prayerful consideration, he wrote an acceptance—wrote it and left his house late one night to put the letter into the post. But it was never posted.

The thing that happened was that a few earnest people, some belonging to his own church, some affiliated with other churches, but all full of ardour for the Kingdom of God, impressed with the ability and enthusiasm of Mr. Meyer, came together and determined to stand by him if only he could be persuaded to remain in Leicester. None of them knew quite what they intended, but they were moved by a common impulse and ready to sustain any effort for the Kingdom of God to which they might be led. They had not yet acquainted Mr. Meyer with their purpose when he went out to post the letter accepting the call to Sheffield. But now mark the crossing of God's lines. My brother-in-law, Arthur Rust, also had the habit of posting letters at the last minute of the day, and he and Meyer met outside the Post Office. What more natural than that Meyer should show his letter and say what it contained ? And though Arthur Rust was not an impulsive man, what else could he do than to tell Meyer what had already happened as to his continued stay in Leicester ? There they stood and looked at each other, the man of business and the preacher of the Gospel ; surely both were conscious of God. Of course, the only way open to Meyer was to remain in Leicester, so the letter was never posted.

The following Saturday evening the group of Adventurers met in the Presbyterian Church, of which Mr. Rutherford, who afterwards became the minister of the Cathedral of Kirkwall, in the Orkney Islands, was then the minister, and as the new venture was to open the following day the whole business was committed to the Great Disposer of Events.

The Sunday services were arranged to be held in the Museum Buildings, where there are some valuable pictures and statuary. An old lady, one of Mr. Meyer's most constant and enthusiastic supporters, had her puritanic instincts shocked when with some others she went to prepare the room : nothing would satisfy her but that she should hurry back to her home, some distance from the town, and bring sheets in which she wrapped the statues and covered several of the pictures. Though it was not intended, this became quite an advertisement, for besides the sermon there were the vestments, and some people came not so much to hear the preacher as to see the figures in their flowing robes.

That same old lady through the years was always her minister's staunch helper and sometimes his embarrassment. She was as energetic as he was. On one occasion hurrying to some meeting she just snatched part of a meal, and trotting out of her house was met by her pastor who was passing at the moment. Of course each stopped. " Friend," said Mr. Meyer, " do you know that your bonnet is on the wrong way ? " " Friend," she instantly answered, " put it on the right way," which, being on easy terms with his people, he proceeded to do.

A quaint wit had that old lady. On her way to Ramsgate on one occasion, she sat in a crowded carriage reading a magazine. A young clergyman in the far corner handed tracts round the compartment, but when he offered one to a minstrel with a banjo and blackened face, it was refused. " I don't believe in God," he shouted. Behind her journal she said, " The fool hath said in his heart, ' There is no God.' " The scoffer turned to her and said, " What ! do you call me a fool ? " Calmly looking over the top of the page she said, " No, I don't, but God does, and you certainly look like one ! " As the train drew up at a station he disappeared and the young curate, somewhat nervous, was profuse in his thanks. This was the lady of the robes.

The services on May 12th, 1878 were even more largely attended than the promoters had hoped. The first sermon was from Ezra viii. 21–23, where the ancient leader tells how he sought a right way for the people and for their little ones, and declares that as a result of the prayer to God " He was intreated of us."

There were not wanting those who declared that Meyer had dwindled down to the rank of a city missionary, and it must have taken some courage to venture out into the open air three times a week summer and winter with such faithful souls as gathered round him, and, after ringing a bell, to hold services, frequently far into the darkness. There were people whom I afterwards met who would show me the chair he stood on. Infirmary Square was the great rendezvous. The Mission that had begun when Mr. Meyer was minister of Victoria Road Church was handed over to him, a little room in a somewhat unsavoury quarter. Paradise Mission, as it was called, witnessed many a scene of grace, and has only now been disbanded because the building was in decay.

After five months the little assembly of believers formed itself into a Church of Christ. Friday, September 23rd, 1878, is the memorable date. Both pastor and people were now burning their boats. Their object was declared to be union in seeking to evangelise the people lying outside ordinary Christian agencies, and it was determined that every member, as far as practicable, should be a worker.

Which reminds us that when Dr. Guthrie visited Mr. Oncken at Hamburg and saw the influence of the Baptists he had gathered around him there since 1834, he asked Oncken how many workers he had, to which came the prompt answer, " Three thousand." Somewhat impatiently Guthrie said, " I did not ask you how many members you had, but how many workers." Still Oncken answered, " Three thousand," but added, " Every member is a worker," much to Dr. Guthrie's delight.

After a year of sporadic work it became clear that a permanent home was needed for the people who were being increasingly interested, and continually increasing in numbers. On March 8th, 1879, definite prayer was offered that, if it was God's will, some distinct token might be given, and some days afterwards a lady whom he was visiting put into Meyer's hand an envelope containing a £10 note, saying that it was to go towards the erection of a new building for his ministry. Not much that for the building of a sanctuary, but giant oaks from little acorns grow, and the acorn was planted.

It grew quickly. Within a fortnight the people themselves had promised £1,770. And still it grew until when the building was complete about £10,000 had been contributed. There was no public canvass for funds, but daily in the house of one of the supporters a few elect souls gathered, and in detail with prayer and supplication with thanksgiving they made their requests known to God.

It seemed almost more difficult to determine the site of the new building than to raise the money for it. The constituency was spread all over the town, and yet it would have been most unwise to plant a church in the centre, where the town was over-churched already. At length a plot of ground beyond the town was chosen, on the plateau on the top of the hill. It was a cabbage garden when it was purchased and for years we were reminded how one evening the people gathered amongst the cabbages and consecrated the site to the Lord.

Then the question of architecture arose. For the unique work there must be a unique building, and one of the plans sent in for competition fulfilled all desires. The auditorium itself was to be rectangular, the roof rising high above it, octangular. Reality marks the construction, there is no make-believe, no camouflage, though that word was then unknown. Wood is wood, brick is brick, stone is stone, iron is iron. There is no wood painted to resemble oak, no brick stuccoed to resemble stone. When the building was opened some thought the interior cold with its brick walls, and that, perhaps, is the first feeling of those who enter it to-day. But it grows on you as you continue to come, and with its one coloured window, ivy covered walls and gilded minaret, it stands, unlike any other structure in

England, but suited in every detail for its intended purpose. There is now an official cathedral in Leicester, but this has been its actual cathedral all along. The Memorial Stones were laid on July 1st, 1880, one of them by Mr. Meyer's father, and the opening services were held in the following year on July 2nd.

The name to be given to the building was much debated. With a sort of prevision it was at length determined to avoid any ecclesiastical title. It was to be neither a church nor a chapel, the latter word a bad mixture of French and Latin. But what then ? A meeting house in imitation of our early Nonconformist forefathers, or a tabernacle following the example of Spurgeon and others ? Neither. Let it be just a hall. It was noticed the people come more readily and are more at ease in a hall than in a place with a grander name. Very well, a hall it shall be. But what shall be its Christian name, so to speak ? Again the vote was for simplicity : the building is in Melbourne Road : let it be Melbourne Hall. Carried unanimously. In after years when I was minister there, and the breach between the old church at Victoria Road and the new church at Melbourne Hall was healed, I used to remind folk that Melbourne is the capital of Victoria !

Melbourne Hall can easily hold a congregation of twelve hundred people, has had two thousand in it, and quite frequently has a crowd of fourteen hundred worshippers. From the beginning it was filled in the evenings, and the morning congregation rapidly increased. In my day, as in Meyer's day, there were generally two rows of chairs down each aisle, and it amused me often, probably amused him, too, though I scarcely think his sense of humour was so strong, when visitors came, their chief recollection was not the sermon, but the wonderful celerity of the seat-stewards in removing the chairs from the aisles ! A humbling reflection for the preacher !

All sorts of meetings were held, beginning with a prayer meeting on Saturdays splendidly sustained. Sunday School classes multiplied in every corner, and there were a vast variety of agencies during the week. The Sunday Schools increased to such an extent that in Meyer's time there were about 2,500 scholars, and even a larger number afterwards, no less than three public Council Schools being rented for the purpose. This implied an army of workers : that has been the strength of Melbourne Hall throughout the years, indeed, the Sunday School teachers alone would have made an encouraging congregation. At one time there were no less than eighty-three meetings, large and small, held each week.

The pressure on the space became at length so great that further accommodation was necessary, and in memory of their father, three brothers, Theodore, Ralph and Robert Walker, erected alongside Melbourne Hall the Walker Memorial Hall, which in its turn proved unable to take the overflow, and in later years a fine series of class-rooms was also added. Rev. C. B. Sawday succeeded Dr. Meyer, the Rev. H. M. Nield succeeded me, and the church to-day is flourishing under the devoted care of Rev. Benjamin Gibbon, its membership being over thirteen hundred ; and as I write a branch church is in process of erection in a suburb still further beyond the city.

Melbourne Hall is Dr. F. B. Meyer's abiding monument. Like himself it is original and real, and, set on a hill, it cannot be hid. He himself writes concerning it, " What Melbourne Hall was and is to those of us who watched every brick added to its rising structure words fail to tell. It is quite unique in its appearance. On winter nights when it is lighted up, it would seem as though some giant, striding across the country, had for a moment set down his huge lantern at the junction of the four roads. Many a wayfarer is cheered in the stormy night by its gleaming welcome."

Rev. George H. McNeal, now minister of the Mother Methodist Church in City Road, London, was for some years associated with Mr. Collier's wonderful work in the Central Hall, Manchester. This was built on the site of a derelict Wesleyan Church in Oldham Street at the instance of Dr. Pope, and Mr. McNeal remembers him saying that it was the building of Melbourne Hall in Leicester by F. B. Meyer that gave him the idea of the hall in Manchester, the first of the great Central Halls now established in all parts of the country, the inauguration of which has been one of the greatest things the Wesleyan Methodist Church has ever achieved.

It is worthy of remark that at the Tuesday midday services in connection with the Manchester Central Hall Dr. Meyer preached no less than seventy-five times!

CHAPTER FIVE

THE HUMAN TOUCH

THE human touch was given to Meyer by a new touch of the Divine. He had been thrown amongst men ever since he resigned his first charge in Leicester : had largely interested himself in Temperance work and had lifted up, on occasion, men from the gutter. The Blue Ribbon Movement claimed him and he rode on the crest of its wave. Not content with public advocacy he laid hold of individuals. With his band of helpers he would see drunken men to their homes of a Saturday night, putting his card in their waistcoat pocket with a message and invitation on it. More than once he put men into the train for some neighbouring town or village when they were incapable of finding their own way. All that.

But there was a restlessness about it all. Like a rider on a bicycle he felt he must go on or else he would go off. He would advise people who came to him to read Andrew Murray's " Abide in Christ " which was then the popular spiritual manual, but he somehow gave the impression as he rushed off that it was second-hand advice. The untiring energy of his nature was always demanding an outlet, he had scarcely learned what Chaucer so pawkily wrote, " He hasteth wel that wyseley can abyde."

All sorts of people came to Melbourne Hall, amongst them Hudson Taylor, and afterwards two of " the Cambridge Seven " who had volunteered for China. By this time, though I was still evangelising with Manton Smith, I had married into a Leicester family, the ceremony taking place in Melbourne Hall, and my headquarters were in Leicester.

I was on my journeys and the Cambridge men occupied our room. Of what happened there Mr. Meyer has himself written.

" The visit of Messrs. Stanley Smith and Studd to Melbourne Hall will always mark an epoch in my own life. Before then my Christian life was spasmodic and fitful ; now flaming up with enthusiasm, and then pacing weariedly over leagues of grey ashes and cold cinders. I saw that these young men had something which I had not, but which was within them a constant source of rest and strength and joy. And never shall I forget a scene at 7 a.m. in the grey November morning, as daylight was flickering into the bedroom, paling the guttered candles which from a very early hour had been lighting up the page of Scripture and revealing the figures of the devoted Bible students, who wore the old cricketing or boating costume of earlier days, to render them less sensible of the raw, damp climate. The talk we held then was one of the most formative influences of my life. Why should I not do what they had done ? Why should I not yield my whole nature to God, working out day by day *that* which He would will and work within ? Why should I not be a vessel, though only of earthenware, meet for the Master's use, because purged and sanctified ?

" There was nothing new in what they told me. They said, that ' A man must not only believe in Christ for final salvation, but must trust Him for victory over every sin, and for deliverance from every care.' They said, that ' The Lord Jesus was willing to abide in the heart which was wholly yielded up to Him.' They said, that ' If there were some things in our lives that made it difficult for us to surrender our whole nature to Christ, yet if we were willing to be made willing to surrender them, He would make us not only willing but glad.' They said, that ' Directly we give or attempt to give ourselves to Him, He takes us.' All this was simple enough. I could have said it myself. But they urged me to take the definite step ; and I shall be for ever thankful that they did. And if in a distant country they should read this page, let them be encouraged to learn that one heart at least has been touched with a new fire, and that one voice is raised in prayer for their increase in the knowledge and love of Him Who has become more real to the suppliant, because of their brotherly words.

" Very memorable was the night when I came to close

quarters with God. The Angel that wrestled with Jacob found me, eager to make me a Prince. There were things in my heart and life which I felt were questionable, if not worse ; I knew that God had a controversy with respect to them ; I saw that my very dislike to probe or touch them was a clear indication that there was mischief lurking beneath. It is the diseased joint that shrinks from the touch and tender eye that shudders at the light. At the same time I did not feel willing to give these things up. It was a long struggle. At last I said feebly, ' Lord, I am willing to be made willing ; I am desirous that Thy will should be done in me and through me, as thoroughly as it is done in Heaven ; come and take me and break me and make me.' That was the hour of crisis, and when it had passed I felt able at once to add, ' And now I give myself to Thee : body, soul and spirit ; in sorrow or in joy ; in the dark or in the light ; in life or in death, to be Thine only, wholly and for ever. Make the most of me that can be made for Thy glory.' No rapture or rush of joy came to assure me that the gift was accepted. I left the place with almost a heavy heart. I simply assured myself that He must have taken that which I had given, and at the moment of my giving it. And to that belief I clung in all the days that followed, constantly repeating to myself the words, ' I am His.' And thus at last the joy and rest entered and victory and freedom from burdening care and I found that He was moulding my will and making it easy to do what I had thought impossible ; and I felt that He was leading me into the paths of righteousness for His name's sake, but so gently as to be almost imperceptible to my weak sight."

Dr. J. H. Jowett recalls the experience to which Dr. Meyer himself often referred. " Dr. Meyer has told us that his early Christian life was marred and his ministry paralysed just because he had kept back one thing from the bunch of keys he had given to the Lord. Every key save one ! The key of one room was kept for personal use, and the Lord shut out. And the effect of the incomplete consecration was found in lack of power, lack of assurance, lack of joy and peace. The joy of the Lord begins when we hand over the last key. We sit with Christ on His throne as soon as we have surrendered all our crowns, and made Him sole and only ruler of our life and its possessions."

This experience was published in a tractate, and soon afterwards at Keswick a fleet of some thirty boats was on Derwentwater when somebody asked Meyer, who was in one of the boats, to recount the experience. I never admired him more than when he answered, " No, no, you cannot live on an experience."

But the outcome of the experience in his own case was an ordered persistent effort to help men, not a spasmodic occasional burst of activity. Already he had some knowledge of the peril which awaits men as they come out of prison. The release of the father of a young girl who attended the services was expected one morning, and he promised to meet him at the prison gate ; but the man did not appear, as he had been transferred to another prison and was set at liberty there. But Meyer waited and saw that almost invariably the released men made for the public house opposite.

His spirit was so stirred that he immediately called on the Governor of the prison and asked if he might be permitted to visit the prisoners morning by morning as they were released from gaol ; and until he left Leicester he was daily to be found there, sometimes before the dawn. He was accustomed to invite his men to the Coffee House a few steps across the road and there lay plans for their future, giving them such help as appeared necessary, or undertaking to be their banker, if they were willing to entrust him with the money given them on their discharge. On one occasion a man declared that he had vowed to have a pint of porter the first morning of his freedom and nothing could persuade him to forego his purpose. Mr. Meyer consented to get him the porter if he would promise to sign the pledge immediately afterwards, and so won the day.

Let him tell the story. " I was in such a position," he writes, " that I did not dare to send any of the men who were at that time assisting me into the public house hard by to get that pint of porter : and I knew there was no one on the premises belonging to the coffee house company that

I could employ for the purpose. And so, as there was nothing else to do, I caught up the first jug that was within reach and sallied forth to the public house at the opposite corner to get this pint of porter. I felt very strange. The barmaid who served me looked at me with such amazement that I think she supposed I had suddenly lost my reason. I assured her however that it was the *final* pint : and explained to her that it was not for myself but for a man in whom I was deeply interested.

" On arriving at my little breakfast party with the jug and glass in my hand, I poured the porter out as quietly as possible without the ' head ' which porter drinkers are accustomed to appreciate. He took the glass and began to drink, and I gave such an unconscious groan that, after two or three efforts, he put down the remainder and said, ' This is the miserablest pint of porter I ever drank. Where's your card, sir ? I may as well sign it as drink any more.' "

The results of this work were immeasurable. It is now in the hands of the Discharged Prisoners' Society, but the personal equation of the parson hurrying from his home in the morning, munching his hurried breakfast on the way, is missing.

Perhaps the unconscious influence we exert will turn out to be the deciding factor of life. " Lord, when saw we Thee ahungered ? " we may, not knowing, ask. At Wairakie in New Zealand, when I saw it, the thermal valley which should have been a mass of verdure was a blackened ruin. The visitor who caused the damage was quite unconscious of the havoc he wrought. Just as he was leaving he dropped a lighted match and left behind him a charred desolation. But there is the unconscious good as well as the unconscious evil, our very aura radiates either bane or blessing. Here is a letter from Mr. Harold H. Pochin, whom I know quite well. It is addressed to Dr. Meyer on September 7th, 1923.

" When I was a little boy of ten years, thirty-six years ago, I was a scholar at the Middle School, Welford Road, Leicester. Every morning for years I passed one coming away from our gaol with one, two, or three of the unfortunate men who had been ' found out ' and just been released. I saw the ' one ' take them into the Welford Coffee House for breakfast, a talk, and a fresh start in life.

" The ' one ' little thought as he passed the boy every morning that a sermon was being preached. I went home one day and said, ' Mother, I wish when I grow up I could be a " Meyer." ' She asked me what I meant, and I told her how I loved the ' one ' for what he did. That ' one ' was you, sir. Last Christmas I visited the Leicester Gaol and recited to the fellows there, and I was in the middle of Kipling's ' If,' saying, ' If you could *wait* and not be tired of waiting ' ; I suddenly thought of the boy of ten that I was, and swiftly it came to me that I was something of a ' Meyer ' : ' the sermon has found its issue. I am—here,' and I was so affected that I almost stopped.

" The boy of ten has had the supreme honour of reciting to upwards of 250,000 men in France and elsewhere, pure clean humour, in the huts, to kill the vulgar filth so rampant these times. I am still doing what I can, but you were a first great influence on me in those deeds of mercy. Please receive my loving thanks."

The attempt at Rescue work invariably leads to the need of preventive work, so the experience amongst the men at the prison gate suggested the desirability of doing something for boys in danger of drifting into a criminal life. Meyer had been so much encouraged by the support given him in one direction that he launched out into the other, rented a house, installed a caretaker and filled it with friendless boys. This became his real home, he was never so delighted as when he was amongst the lads, and he proved a real father to some of them. " Providence House " holds happy memories for some men even to-day.

God always rewards anything done in His name. Not in the coin of this earthly realm, however, sometimes quite the reverse, but always in the currency of His Own Kingdom. The reward for sacrifice is further sacrifice ; of service more service. One need met revealed another. How to help unskilled men out of work ? The immediate remedy appeared to be the sale of firewood. That meant wood chopping, hatchets, saws, and accommodation. These were provided. But how was the firewood to be sold? The problem was solved, and one morning Leicester was astonished to see a van in its streets, with the legend on it, " F. B. Meyer, Firewood Merchant." People bought the bundles out of sheer sympathy, perhaps not unmixed with amusement. Gipsy Smith boasts that he was once a timber merchant, when as a boy he sold skewers, but Meyer can more than match him. He himself was as proud of his new departure as a boy with a new toy. Not only had he a van but he possessed a horse, and on one occasion, when some Sunday scholars had a picnic in the country, he actually borrowed a saddle and rode out to them on his own steed, his trousers tucked up to his knees before he arrived at his destination. That was great fun.

" Another incident stands out clear cut before me," he wrote. " I had been led to take up the work at the prison gate, stationing myself there each morning to receive and greet the prisoners as they came out, taking them to breakfast with me and afterwards helping them to determine on their future life. The great need had constantly presented itself to me of establishing an industrial home, where they might reside under Christian influences, whilst at the same time they maintained themselves and paid their way by their work. In a small way I had already commenced wood-chopping, but the need for larger premises was urgent. A large disused yard, shedding and dwelling house had recently come under my notice, the rent of which was £100 per annum, besides all the outlay consequent on preparing it for my purpose. It was offered me under a three years' agreement and I very much hesitated. I did not like to ask the help of others, being assured that if my Heavenly Father wanted me to undertake it *He* would be sufficient. The question, however, was—What did *He* wish and intend ?

" With my heart opened to Him, that He might impress it with His will, as of old the Urim and Thummim stone shone or dimmed with His Yea and Nay, I turned to my

Bible, and was led to this verse, which burnt itself into my innermost soul : ' Peter answered and said, " Lord, if it be Thou, bid me come unto Thee on the water." And He said, " Come." ' It seemed as though Jesus Himself were in the heart of the new difficulties to which He was calling me, and as though in answer to my repeated challenge, ' Lord, is it Thou ? and if it be, bid me come,' He was perpetually replying, with the sublime, all-inclusive answer, ' Come.' I took the place, signed the agreement, carried on the firewood business for three years—though amid continued opposition—and finally came out of it, on my removal to London, without a halfpenny loss, but with invaluable experience and a consciousness of a wealth of blessing and help that had accrued to scores of men, some of whom keep in touch with me to this day."

He often had Saturday dinner at New Parks, my wife's home, and always joined the family on Christmas Day. But when he had his own family of boys this Christmas visit to us, now at Regent Road, was of short duration. He would hurry from the table to a cab that came for him, go round a dozen houses picking up a joint there, a pudding here, pork pies round the corner, a ham over the way, nuts and crackers from this friend, almonds and raisins from that, until there was just room left for him to get in and drive in triumph to Providence House. He would let nobody else do this for him, the provender must not be sent to the Home, the joints were to be hot early on Christmas afternoon and were to be personally collected—all that was part of the ritual, and if report speaks truly the boys had afterwards a very hilarious time, while those who had given the food enjoyed their evening all the more. But he gave himself !

A " Window Cleaning Brigade " was the next venture, and men with " F. B. Meyer " on their hats wheeled two long ladders through the town and did a good business. It can be imagined that all this cost much in thought and time and money. Each morning there were prayers at Providence House, the visit to the prison, the conferences

at the Coffee House, and then the usual minister's work for
the day. Money came as it was needed, sometimes there
was a hard push, expecially one morning when he needed
£100 and did not know where to get it. Of all mornings
the first letter he opened that morning contained a cheque
for £100! Let those who doubt God's care explain—
Why that? Why then? And for that matter, why
anything?

CHAPTER SIX

THE MOVING FINGER WRITES

MELBOURNE HALL became a centre as well as a sphere. All sorts of people visited the church, representing a wide variety of Christian effort. It became, in fact, the Church of the Cordial Welcome, and as a consequence a place of pilgrimage and a centre of evangelical and missionary influence in Leicester and far beyond. As a result the minister of the church became widely known and began to be sought after.

The Keswick Trustees, always open-eyed for men with a message, heard of the new uprising of spiritual influence and invited Mr. Meyer to the Convention. As customary he was not at first asked to speak, but as an honoured guest he inhaled the Keswick atmosphere and that prepared him for his share in the programme the following year. Mr. Meyer had attended other gatherings of a similar nature in previous years, had shared as a learner in the historic Conventions at Oxford and Brighton out of which the Keswick Convention sprang, had been a guest at Broadlands where a notable company of people debated what some thought to be the new doctrine of Perfection, and again had joined another group which Archdeacon Wilberforce invited to Southampton. All of these had left distinct impressions on the life of the young minister, but none of them brought him triumphant faith. That was left for the Keswick visit in 1887. Again he himself must tell of his lonely vigil on the hills when the new vision was granted.

" Before I first spoke on the platform I had my own deeper experience, on a memorable night when I left the little town with its dazzling lamps, and climbed the neighbouring hill. As I write the summer night is again casting its spell on me. The light clouds veil the stars and pass. The breath of the mountains leads me to yearn for a fresh intake of God's Spirit. May we not count on the Anointing Spirit to grant us a fresh infilling when we are led to seek it ? May we not dare to believe that we have received, even when there is no answering emotion ? Do we not receive by faith ? These were the questions which a few of us had debated far into the night, at a prayer meeting convened at which a number of men were agonizing for the Spirit.

" I was too tired to agonize, so I left that prayer meeting and as I walked I said, ' My Father, if there is one soul more than another within the circle of these hills that needs the gift of Pentecost it is I : I want the Holy Spirit but I do not know how to receive Him and I am too weary to think, or feel, or pray intensely.' Then a Voice said to me, ' As you took forgiveness from the hand of the dying Christ, take the Holy Ghost from the hand of the living Christ, and reckon that the gift is thine by a faith that is utterly indifferent to the presence or absence of resultant joy. According to thy *faith* so shall it be unto thee.' So I turned to Christ and said, ' Lord, as I breathe in this whiff of warm night air, so I breathe into every part of me Thy blessed Spirit.' I felt no hand laid on my head, there was no lambent flame, there was no rushing sound from heaven : but by *faith*, without emotion, without excitement, I took, and took for the first time, and I have kept on taking ever since.

" I turned to leave the mountain side, and as I went down the tempter said I had nothing, that it was all imagination, but I answered, ' Though I do not feel it, I reckon that God is faithful.' "

His hostess tells that that night she was sitting up for him and he came in greatly agitated and began walking up and down the room in deep self-examination ; again and again he said, " Can I have been wrong and wanting until now ? Has my life hitherto been lacking in power ? " They prayed together, and he retired without joy, but the next morning all was peace. Later he wrote, " That was high water mark ! Alas that tides like that should ever drop down to the beach ! "

When he became a speaker at Keswick he instantly approved himself as supplying a need on the platform, he was less theological and didactic than the others, more human and sympathetic. He at once became a leader, and in the numerous Conferences in various parts of the country that followed his ministry he led many into the rest of faith.

He now became increasingly concerned that his fellow-ministers should share the Grace that had come to him. So in a letter in this same year to *The Baptist* he invited them to unite in prayer in the early morning of each Lord's Day " to seek a fuller enduement of the power of the Holy Spirit for themselves and their brethren." There was a considerable response and so the Baptist Ministers' Prayer Union came into being with Rev. George Wainwright of Manchester as its first Secretary. It was decided to hold Conferences and Retreats for the members of the Prayer Union, and the first assembled in Melbourne Hall on November 23rd and 24th, when about seventy ministers were present. Owing to the illness of the first Secretary, Rev. J. J. Martin of Erith was called to the post in April, 1888, and still occupies it. The membership steadily increased until it reached considerably over eight hundred, and in January, 1908, it became amalgamated with the Baptist Ministers' Fraternal Union, and the last published list shows a membership of nearly six hundred.

In a farewell letter to the Fraternal Union, dated Sunday, March 10th, 1929, he refers to " the life which is hidden with Christ in God, which receives its constant incentive and power from the Vine, which is anointed by Pentecost for service, which moves Society. My one regret to-day is that I must now carry my bat to the pavilion and see others play the game. But this is the Master-stroke."

Toward the end of 1887 a call came from Regent's Park Church urging him to become its minister. It seemed impossible to relinquish the church in Leicester that he had built up, equally impossible to stay. They sent him off to

Algeria for three weeks, which to him were like Paul's three years in the desert of Arabia. He returned home in time for the Christmas services, with his purpose set to sever the bonds that bound him to Leicester, and to undertake the work in London.

The church at Regent's Park was housed in a commodious building, the entrance to which was in the middle of a terrace of dwelling-houses, almost indistinguishable from them. At first it had been designed for a Panorama, but under the influence of Sir Morton Peto and others had been transformed into a church. Dr. Landels was its first minister, and under his pastorate a great West End congregation was gathered : the Rev. David Davies followed and maintained its traditions : when he removed to Hove the church turned to the Leicester minister then rising into considerable prominence in the country, and were successful in their overtures.

Writing to the Ministers' Prayer Union he says, " It is an exchange that will involve prodigious exertions, at a time when I was anticipating some relief from an incessant and prolonged strain : and whatever happens in London it will be very different from that quiet blessed intimacy between Pastor and people which is possible in a country town.

" The Church at Regent's Park have acted with the utmost kindness. First in their cordial invitation ; then in waiting three months ; in assenting to my most stringent conditions, and again in spite of them, in asking me enthusiastically and unanimously to be their Pastor. I hope you will pray for me, from the commencement of my ministry there on the first Sunday in February."

Leicester with common consent regretted Mr. Meyer's departure, and a sum of £400 was promptly subscribed as a token of its high esteem. The Mayor, Sir Thomas Wright, presided at the Farewell Meeting, and so he was bidden a very tearful farewell. The only alleviation was that London was not far from Leicester and that he might therefore often be seen in the scene of his old labours.

It is difficult to say whether at this juncture he was

better known as Meyer of Leicester or as F. B. Meyer of
The Christian. While at Leicester he had published two series
of sermons on Scripture biography in a magazine which is
now extinct, called *The Church;* one, " The Story of Jacob
Retold," the second, " From the Pit to the Throne, the
Story of Joseph." These were revised and appeared weekly
in *The Christian,* attracting wide attention and beginning
that series of Bible Biographies that has become famous all
over the world.

His movements had by this time become so incessant
that it was prophesied even by his best friends that he would
certainly kill himself in a few years. Sir William Robertson
Nicoll, as Claudius Clear, wrote an article in *The British
Weekly,* entitled, " The Devil disguised as a Railway Train,"
which had special reference to Mr. Meyer, and an oblique
application to Dr. Jowett who was at that time also in
danger of wearing himself out in meeting the demands of his
admirers. But Meyer unconcernedly kept on his way :
he had discovered that he could sleep in the train and arrive
quite refreshed for the next day's labour. Although he was
able to enjoy a good meal, he confined himself to Spartan
diet and had learned in a very true sense to " endure
hardness as a good soldier of Jesus Christ." He had great
power of concentration, could easily turn from one task to
the next, and be at his best in both : motion with him
seemed to imply very little friction. Just a little while
before his departure he said to a friend that he thought he
was " an example of what the Lord could do with a man
who concentrated on one thing at a time."

His calm manner was not the sleep of an inactive mind,
it was more like the sleep of a spinning top. Speed rested
him. Once in the library of Sir William Robertson Nicoll,
to revert to him again, he told his host how he envied him his
immense library, how greatly he wished he might have
leisure to browse among the books, when Sir William rather
unkindly spoilt his exclamations of delight by saying,
" Now you know, Meyer, you would not be here an hour
before you would be asking for a Bradshaw's Railway

Guide !'' at which they both heartily laughed. Another
writer, without knowing this incident, spoke of him as
'' St. Francis with a Bradshaw.''

Even in his railway journeys he was not inactive. In
Reveries and Realities he expresses gratitude that he had
never been in a railway accident, nor ever met a case of
incivility on the part of railway employees. It would be
rather difficult indeed to imagine any railway man being
rude to a man with such a benign countenance. He was
always ready to bear witness for his Master if an opportunity
presented itself ; sometimes he wrote in the train, often he
read, frequently he just sat still, and of course at night he
slept. All the prophets were wrong, he did not kill himself
by his journeyings, he just died of having lived, and he was
never in a hurry because he always was in haste.

He was like Wesley, who divided his life into spaces of
five minutes, and chided himself if one of them passed into
idleness. Once Meyer on a speaking tour in Wales with
Dr. Charles Brown, and exhausting him with his activity,
told him that his motto was :

> '' Give every flying minute
> Something to keep in store.''

It almost seemed as if he himself would like to fly with the
minutes. Indeed, during the great strike he did fly to Paris
to keep an engagement, and astonished his secretary by
sending a message that he meant to fly back again ; at his
age and with his heart a very daring experiment.

This haste in living and economy of time made his
friendships rather fugitive. Though he always gave undivided
attention at the moment to the matter in hand, there was
a sense that he would soon be off to something else, and
confidences in which we can shelter do not ripen like Jonah's
gourd. This after all is only a matter of comparison. To
quote the legend on a sundial, '' Life is too slow for those who
wait ; too swift for those who fear ; too long for those who
grieve ; too short for those who rejoice. But for those that
love there is eternity.''

CHAPTER SEVEN

THE SWINGING PENDULUM

REGENT'S PARK CHURCH AND CHRIST CHURCH

On Mr. Meyer's advent to London he had an experience which is probably unique in the history of any minister—four pastorates but only two churches. As we have seen, he came to Regent's Park Church in 1888. After four years there Dr. Newman Hall, of Christ Church, Westminster Bridge Road, made overtures to him, and in 1892 he went to the other side of the Thames, returning, as we shall see presently, to Regent's Park in 1909, and in 1915 again becoming pastor of Christ Church, Westminster Bridge Road. When he passed over the responsibility to Dr. W. C. Poole in 1921 he was appointed Minister Emeritus. In this chapter we shall make a brief survey of these four pastorates, and afterwards chronicle the important events that characterised the forty-one years' ministry in London.

In his first address in the Regent's Park Manual for 1888 he truly says, " The difficulties before us are of no ordinary kind, yet with God's assured blessing I am exceedingly hopeful of seeing the place renew its youth and become again the thriving centre of Christian activity and the spiritual home of thousands. A united handful of people ; a noble building ; a glorious Gospel ; a divine Spirit ; these are ours, and they are the guarantee of ultimate success."

The following year he was able to express encouragement and gratitude. " It is gratifying to see the marked improvement in early attendance on the services," and he urges upon the people the need of consecrated wealth and of

71

proportionate giving. " But let none of these things be done simply as a matter of duty. It is of little use being at the circumference of life if the central heart is not consecrated entirely to Him, who bought us to be His slaves for ever. When shall we learn the lesson that we are not our own, but that our character, our earnings, our time and abilities, our activities and leisure hours are the purchased possession of the Son of God. Only when we have learnt this primary lesson and assumed our true attitude, and given ourselves entirely to the Saviour shall we be truly happy and useful."

In 1890 these are cheering words :—" It is impossible to refrain from reviewing the two first years of my ministry with deep thankfulness. To me it is a matter of perpetual amazement that so much has been accomplished, in spite of many deficiencies and mistakes on the part of your minister." He urges the church to do more for the district, to visit the homes of the people, and closes with a very tender paragraph addressed to the sick and aged. " They are the night-watch, the choristers and intercessors who maintain the unbroken Psalm and the ceaseless Prayer."

In the review of the third year it is said, " There is a greater infusion of the social spirit among us, but there is always room for its growth : and I hope the time is not far distant when we shall be united in one great family circle, each possessing a different temperament and different endowments from the rest, but all animated with the spirit of patient tolerance and divine charity. The stream of fresh-comers amongst us is so incessant that our church temperature is apt to become lowered and tepid unless continually maintained. Once more we go forward, not knowing what may await us, but strong in hope, in faith, and prayer, that God would crowd into this fourth year of my pastorate as much blessing as has been spread over the other three."

In January, 1892, reviewing the past two months, the verdict is, " It has been a great year, whether we consider the money that has been raised or the work that has been accomplished. The renovation of our Sanctuary was most successfully carried out, and it often seems to me, as I see it in the evening, radiant with the electric light, and filled with people, as beautiful a Sanctuary as I could desire. It would be difficult to explain to you how much I love the very fabric in which we spend some of the best hours of our lives : and in this I want you all increasingly to share. It is our holy and beautiful house."

" The visit of Mr. Fullerton gave us an impetus at the beginning of the year, but besides this there has been a steady influx of new members into the church, and every sign that God is using His Word. As a Church we must take a leading part in the Centenary of the Baptist Missionary Society ; and in the Presidency of the London Baptist Association it will be my turn to build a chapel somewhere in the metropolis, and it is in my heart to select the site somewhere in the East End."

But this hope was not fulfilled, for the unforeseen happened. To his fellow-ministers Mr. Meyer, in July 1892, explained the change. " Many of you are doubtless aware that I have received an invitation, the unanimity and heartiness of which has startled me, to become the successor of the Rev. Newman Hall, D.D., at Christ Church. The acceptance of this call will involve no sacrifice of principle on my part, as they are willing to provide a Baptistery and to accede to other conditions which involve my principles."

" My work here is very prosperous, under the Divine blessing. The chapel is filled to the doors, the seats in the area are all appropriated, and a large number of agencies are in vigorous operation, whilst the tide of additions to the membership has never ebbed. And yet I feel that it is God's will that I should retire from it, and hand it over as ' a going concern ' to my successor, whom I believe the great Head of the Church will provide. Two considerations largely influence me. Though my convictions as to the truth of Believer's Baptism were never stronger, yet I am less of a denominationalist than ever : and though I quite admit that denominations fulfil a useful function, I do not feel that my special function lies in that direction, but that I can best serve my generation from an undenominational standpoint.

" In addition to this I desire to devote myself more largely to the service of the masses, which I cannot do so well as long as I have to respond to the many outside claims which the pastorate of this church involves : but for which I shall have abundant opportunity in my new charge.

" I am quite aware that my decision may involve misunderstanding and surprise. I cannot help this. The cloud seems clearly moving and I must follow it, and I must leave my vindication in the hands of that Master Whose slavery is perfect freedom."

To his people at Regent's Park he wrote, " The question has presented itself to me thus. Shall I devote the remaining years of my manhood to the service of a section of the Church of Christ, or accept a position that is equally in touch with all sections of Evangelical Christians ? And the whole drift of my past life and work has pointed to the inevitable conclusion that I can only give one answer to that question and accept the latter alternative.

" I have often questioned whether I was acting consistently with my deepest principles, to be officiating as the minister of an influential and successful church, drawing a large salary, and surrounded by every sign of success, and welcomed in all parts of the country as a popular preacher, whilst the great masses of the people were living in sin and need in the more densely populated districts of London. An opportunity is now presented to me of fulfilling a long cherished purpose, and I want to engage in it with the feeling that you freely give me up to it and yield me your sympathy and your prayers."

Whether they freely gave him up or not may be judged by some extracts from the Prefatory Notes to the Regent's Park Church Year Book. " The year 1892 marks an epoch in the history of our Church. The commencement was shadowed by no foreboding : no fears were entertained that the then Pastor, the Rev. F. B. Meyer, would have left us before the year was out : hopes were high, and hearts and hands were strong : new members were still being enrolled on the books of the Church in a stream which commenced three years before : and Pastors, officers and people were thanking God and taking courage for further activity, and looking forward hopefully to another year of progress and aggressive effort against the ever-present force of sin and unbelief.

" Before many months were over, however, rumours in the religious papers suggested that Mr. Meyer was not unlikely to leave Regent's Park for another sphere of work in another part of London—rumours which, at first derided as absurd, soon proved to be only too well grounded : and in July, 1892, Mr. Meyer announced that he had accepted an invitation to become the Pastor of Christ Church, Westminster. The announcement was received with regret and dismay, but having been delivered as a final decision, no choice was left to the church but to accept it, and in September Mr. Meyer bade farewell to the church at Regent's Park and entered upon his new charge in South London.

" We would not forget the valued services which Mr. Meyer rendered during his four years' ministry amongst us, not only to raise the cause of the Lord Jesus Christ in the world, by means of the many men and women whom he was the means of bringing to the knowledge of God, but also to our Church in building it up and setting on foot several agencies to help in extending the Kingdom of Jesus in the neighbourhood. He has gone to work elsewhere, and we pray God that his work may be blessed in ever greater measure than it was amongst us."

Neither to his fellow-ministers nor to his Church did Mr. Meyer disclose all his motives ; quite likely they were hidden from his own consciousness, and the secrecy with which the arrangements were carried through may almost be taken as evidence of this. He was so determined on the step that he dared not risk the pressure that would have been surely brought to bear on him had he consulted the Church or even conferred with its officers. In fact, he was sure of his purpose but he was not sure of himself, and more than once in his life he safeguarded his action in the same way.

In America, on one occasion, there was a man so impressed with his teaching that he followed him to the next city where he was to speak, and took a room in the hotel where he was to stay, in order to see whether he lived up to the high standard he set before other people. He had his meals at the next table and observed him in all possible ways, and at the end he burst into the study of Dr. Curtis Lee Laws and declared that he had failed in no particular. Many others bear similar testimony. In the feminine virtues Meyer was as near negative and positive perfection as it is given to man to attain, but the broad masculine virtues (if a distinction can be drawn between the two, and if the adjectives are allowed), though present, were not so conspicuous. He would have been the first to admit it, and in stating it plainly I do not yield to any one in my admiration of him. Like Cromwell he would say, " Paint me, wart and all."

The magnificent pile of buildings known as Christ Church, which Newman Hall planned and erected at the junction of Westminster Bridge Road and Kennington Road, was an attraction Meyer could not resist. As a young man he had seen its growth ; had known of the change from Surrey Chapel in Blackfriars Road, where Rowland Hill had begun his ministry ; had admired its Gothic grandeur, the great Lincoln Tower, the gift of Newman Hall's American admirers ; and Hawkstone Hall, so suitable for smaller meetings ; and early impressions inevitably affect the whole after life.

Newman Hall had fulfilled his ambition in the erection of this stately church : his hope had been that, though it was on the south side of the river, it was near enough Westminster Abbey to become the Cathedral of Nonconformity, and being attached to no denomination and having a revised liturgy, that it might embrace all sections of the Church of Christ—hence the name. But he had to learn that East and West in the world are not more surely separated than London north and south of the Thames. It might almost be said that " North is north and south is south, and never the twain shall meet." It is singular, but it is true. The Wesleyans have done better in erecting their Central Hall on the north side, under the very shadow of the Abbey, and the Roman Catholics in choosing the Westminster site for their Cathedral. There is a small Christ Church, too, in Westminster, but Christ Church beyond the Thames, even with the new London County Hall on the same side, is still in a backwash. Dr. Poole, the present minister, is to be congratulated on the large measure of his success. Whether the tide will ever flow in its direction is very doubtful. Possibly things may alter when Charing Cross Railway Station is moved across the river.

It was my privilege years ago to travel with Newman Hall. He and I, one Sunday afternoon, conducted a service on Calvary, outside the City Wall : we were together at Damascus and Baalbek, sailed from Beyrout to Constantinople, landing at Cyprus, passing Patmos in company ; and in a moment of confidence he opened his heart as to the frustration of his great effort. " Had I my time over again," he said, " with my present knowledge, I would build a Workmen's Hall at Westminster and use the surplus money to build three or four churches in the suburbs of London."

If I might have interpreted Meyer to himself, I think it would have been right to say that he had a worthy ambition to solve the insoluble problem. It looked as if he might succeed. He had experience of the people in Leicester, he had been a successful minister in the west of London, he was *persona grata* with a great body of Anglicans, he had a growing reputation in England, and he had made a very deep impression on the Evangelical life of America. He would at least make trial of the situation, and he was so set on it, so much attracted by its difficulty, so fearful lest something might prevent him, and at the bottom a little ashamed of his desertion of Regent's Park, that he practically accepted the new church before he informed the old one. It says a good deal both for him and the church that after a lapse of years he went back to it again.

On the first Sunday in October he began his ministry in the new sphere, and from 1892 to 1902 he as nearly succeeded in raising Christ Church to the front rank as it was possible, even went beyond his friends' highest dreams. We will leave to another chapter the full estimate of the work, content here to note that he devoted himself to it with all his energy and enthusiasm, carrying forward the immense Sunday School work centred in the church, making a definite and largely rewarded effort to reach the slums of the neighbourhood, actually living at the church each week from Saturday evening until Monday morning, having a bath and a wardrobe bed fitted into one of the vestries, glorying in the splendid Sanctuary of which he was proud to be minister, and putting new ardour into much of the work of the other churches of South London. He came to Christ Church the year Spurgeon died, and in the unrest that followed at the Metropolitan Tabernacle it was no wonder that a considerable number of its former members migrated to the new ministry.

But on September 30th, 1901, he addressed a letter to the church :

" To speak quite simply, I do not feel able to continue to give to Christ Church the minute and special care which it must have if it is to be efficiently maintained. Neither nervously nor physically can I bear the severe and constant strain which is involved in such a Pastorate, together with the outside work to which I feel I am specially called. And if I must choose, I am led to think that I had better consecrate what strength and time are left to me to the latter service which may, by God's blessing, prove of widespread benefit to the whole Church of Christ.

" In September of next year I shall have completed *ten* years of ministry at Christ Church, and thirty-five of Pastoral work : and I propose during that month to resign the charge which has been so blessed and happy, that I may quietly travel through the world, and especially through Great Britain, Ireland and the Colonies, and the United States, doing what I can to quicken and raise the standard of Christian living.

" Naturally I cling to a fixed Pastorate, and especially to my beautiful Church. It will be a real wrench to tear myself away and only a sense of duty compels me. I think, also, that it is better to give up my Pastorate while our congregations are larger than ever, and the whole organisation thoroughly healthy.

" In the meanwhile I want to assist in securing the best man possible as my successor : and if we are not able to find one at the time I have mentioned, I will gladly retain the nominal Pastorate till the Church is settled.

" The officers have earnestly entreated me to reconsider my resignation, but I am sure it is wisest and best to adhere to it : and at the age of fifty-five I may yet do real service to the whole Church of Christ.

" P.S. Don't let us talk too much about it, but bend our strength to the best winter campaign we have ever had. God has a David somewhere."

But the intention of retirement in 1902 was not carried out. It was not found possible to secure such a pastor as the church desired. So arrangements were made with Dr. A. T. Pierson to undertake the duties of the pulpit for two prolonged periods and thus free Mr. Meyer for wider ministry.

Writing from Stockholm to his Assistant Minister, Rev. A. W. Evans, he says on October 7th, 1902 :

" I am so thankful about the success of the Thursday service, and for the splendid congregations, and for the many tidings of benefit being received. Do tell the people on Sunday what pleasure all this gives to me and how I am hoping to hear of a deep work of revival throughout all our organisations.

" I am glad also that Dr. Pierson is moving about altering the evening service. If it can be done I shall be only too thankful. When the question was raised before, I thought the tenure of my Pastorate would be short, and therefore was quite willing to let the majority settle it. But under the existing circumstances I think that Dr. Pierson is very wise in moving in the matter. And if he succeeds in achieving the alteration I shall certainly stand by it.

" Here in Stockholm I have had the honour and pleasure of being introduced to the Queen, who came to a Bible reading at

Prince Bernadotte's. She kindly said, ' I look upon you as an old friend, as I have read your books.' "

Another letter written on April 9th, 1907, to Mr. Evans, who had by that time undertaken the oversight of a church at Malvern, may be quoted :

" Please thank your people very warmly and accept my thanks yourself for your loving birthday greetings. Yesterday, my sixtieth birthday, was full of love and congratulation, but to me rather sad. First because of the shadow of departure from the people whom I love : and next because of my deep consciousness that I might have done better. But this *stepping into* the grave to be there *with Christ* is probably the path to the most fruitful *time of my life. May it be so !* "

The pendulum swung again, and in September, 1909, we find Mr. Meyer back at Regent's Park Chapel. The Year Book of that year says, " At the time when the last review was written, the prospect for our church did not appear bright : the possibility of a pastoral interregnum dragging on for many months could not be lightly faced. Yet in the Review there was a note of confidence, shared, we trust, by the church members as well as the officers, that God had yet bright days in store for the old church we love.

" To-day the members of the church join with us, its officers, in devout thankfulness to Him Who hath thus further ' blessed us on our way ' by bringing back to us Rev. F. B. Meyer, our Pastor of former years (1888–1892) to be the under-shepherd in charge of this fold, representing one small section of the one great flock of the divine Shepherd.

" ' Now thank we all our God ' is the refrain of this Review. A year ago we looked into an uncertain future—into the dark : to-day we rejoice that after six months of waiting and anxiety, the darkness has passed and a sense of rest has come with the knowledge that our Heavenly Father has placed here, as His light-bearer, a man who, through so many years—not alone in one denomination or in one country—with indomitable energy and consecrated earnestness, has borne such signal witness to the Light.

" The story of Mr. Meyer's coming to us is easily told. From April to September he was away on extended mission tour from Turkey to China. But we had reason to believe that he was feeling the strain of this peripatetic work, and we were able, by correspondence, to secure his services for our church for the autumn months. At the end of September the church invited him to become its Pastor, and in a few weeks we rejoiced to know that he had come, not to ' supply ' but to stay. It is hardly necessary to state in words that the congregations have increased greatly, and that a considerable number have already joined the church, and that God's presence has already been made manifest."

In the Year Book for 1912, Dr. Meyer writes, " The personnel of our congregations is continually changing. People from all parts of the country, our Empire, and the world, come and go : but we realise the great opportunity of such a situation, and we are glad to scatter seeds that may be borne by the living streams to all parts. We must always be on the alert to entertain strangers, and especially to discover and welcome young men and women who have come up to London to make their way.

" In the great public questions of the day we have endeavoured to bear our witness to truth and righteousness : but those themes are to be preferred that bear on the upbuilding of character and the ingathering of the undecided and unsaved. Our success in these latter aspects of our work depends as much on the prayers of the people as the words of the minister. Therefore the incessant appeal of the Apostle is ours—' Brethren, pray for us.' "

In 1913 we read, " The period which has elapsed since I last addressed you has been a very strenuous one, and I am deeply indebted to you for your patience, forbearance and sympathy in the many important matters that have demanded my help. It is impossible to explain to you the interest and thankfulness and incentive which our mutual relationship gives me, or how often I turn to my preparations to serve you with the sense of relief and joy."

In 1914 this :—" The part which we have taken in raising

the Sustentation Fund is especially noteworthy. It is simply amazing to realise that we have contributed *Five Thousand Guineas*, besides the proceeds of the Manse Boxes and the contributions to the Bazaar. Your Pastor is very proud of you and thankful to God for your noble gifts. He also, as you know, has been called to render much time and strength in the same cause : and though this has interfered in many ways with the service needed by such a church and congregation as ours, you have not complained.

"During some weeks at the close of the year I was compelled to take an entire rest, but you were very kind and patient, and I cannot forget the many considerate actions and expressions that brightened those shadowed days."

The reference in the last paragraph is to a sudden illness which overtook Dr. Meyer one Sunday morning, when he fainted in the pulpit. After his rest at Tunbridge Wells and at Pembury in his sisters' home he was able again to take up the threads of work, but with a distinct warning that he must go slower. Happily a call to Rev. F. C. Spurr, of Melbourne, Australia, just before the war in 1914, to become co-pastor, had met with a cordial acceptance, and he carried forward the work with vigour during his colleague's convalescence ; and when Dr. Meyer again accepted the pastorate of Christ Church, Mr. Spurr at an exceptionally attended church meeting on April 15th, was offered a unanimous invitation to the sole pastorate of the church, and accepted it, continuing his valued ministry until by its arbitrary action the Commissioners of Woods and Forests, to whom the site belonged, demanded such extortionate rent that the only alternative was the scattering of the congregation and the dissolution of the church in May, 1922.

So the pendulum swung again, and Dr. Meyer, having twice served as Pastor of Regent's Park Church, went for the second time to Christ Church. He began there on the first Sunday in May, 1915, and was sole minister until 1921. During his absence Dr. John McNeill had had the oversight of the church for a year, and Dr. Len Broughton succeeded McNeill in 1912, making many changes which involved the church in considerable liability ; it was a courageous thing for Dr. Meyer to step into the vacancy caused by his resignation when he returned to America. But he shouldered the burden bravely, and during his early years succeeded in raising enough money to meet the debt, no less than £8,000, and though, in the war-time, he was scarcely as greatly encouraged as in his previous pastorate, nor able to put as much vigour into its various institutions, he did a very notable piece of work during the years that remained.

But now we must retrace our steps and pick up some of the dropped threads.

CHAPTER EIGHT

AS A BAPTIST

DR. MEYER was a convinced Baptist, was always ready to avow his faith, and at several periods of his ministry he did notable service for his own denomination. His little booklet, " Seven Reasons for Believer's Baptism," has had a circulation of 268,000 and has helped a multitude of people. " The longer I live," he says, " the more impressed I am with the beauty and significance of Believer's Baptism, and I cannot but feel that if it were thoroughly understood by Christian people, they would not hesitate to obey the Lord's command. Indeed, they would be eager to pass through the simple outward rite which would express their desire to be as like Him as they may. But remember at the outset," he adds, " that you may be baptized, as a believer, without becoming a member of the Baptist denomination. You may be baptized, and still continue in communion with that Christian body with which you have been accustomed to worship. This rite is a personal matter between the Lord and the individual believer."

Probably no man has baptized more members of other churches, some of them very prominent members, than he. " Even if there were only the faintest possibility of Believer's Baptism being the Master's will, I would be baptized," he adds, " in order to be on the safe side. He will never find fault with those who did all they thought to be His will, even though they had slighter grounds for thinking so than we have for Believer's Baptism. He may find serious fault with those who did not investigate His commandments for themselves, or postponed obedience because the matter was non-essential. True love knows no difference between the essential and the non-essential."

A companion pamphlet entitled, " Seven Reasons for Joining the Church," which has reached its sixty-fifth thousand, has also been most useful. " How greatly the idea of co-operation is growing in these days," he exclaims. " The Church is the great Co-operative Society, under the Inspiration and Guidance of the Holy Spirit." And so he tells us we should join the Church because in that way we shall do better work in the world.

When he undertook the pastorate of Christ Church he insisted on the provision of a baptistery, and it became quite a usual thing for members of the Anglican Church to seek baptism at his hands there. The Rev. George Grubb was amongst the number. It is scarcely a secret to say that the building of a baptistery in Lambeth Parish Church, one of the few Anglican churches in England to make such provision, was prompted by the demand made by Church of England members on Christ Church, and I believe it is correct to say that Mr. Meyer lent his gown to the Rector for his first baptism, and instructed him as to the method of baptizing grown persons.

We have already seen that before he came to London he was instrumental in forming " The Baptist Ministers' and Missionaries' Prayer Union." A companion Prayer Union for the Wives of Ministers and Missionaries, which is still in being with Mrs. James Spurgeon as Secretary, was also formed at Regent's Park Chapel on October 29th, 1890.

One of his earliest experiences when he shared in the meetings of the Baptist Union, was in the Autumn Session at Portsmouth in 1895. Dr. Pentecost had consented to preach the missionary sermon in the Town Hall, and seizing the opportunity to make a great pronouncement, he brought his foolscap sheets, and beginning with Genesis he traced the missionary idea right through the Bible. It was an excellent essay, but a wearisome sermon. The audience began to fade away after the first half hour, but he still went on. In an hour's time half the people were gone.

In the hotel where the leaders were lodged one came in after the other and reported that the sermon was still in progress. Dr. Clifford, with rare courtesy, stayed until the end, and when he arrived he reported that the sermon was finished but the Hall was almost empty

Mr. Meyer was to speak early the next morning for the Prayer Union, and he had already got into the habit of travelling late at night. As a consequence he did not hear the missionary sermon, nor hear of it. He rose to speak the next morning unconscious of the happening of the night before, and at once plunged into his favourite topic of the moment, the work of the Holy Spirit. In his own impressive style he asked the question, " What did Pentecost mean ? " and was greatly surprised when the assembly, instead of being solemnized, burst into laughter. They felt that none of them could answer the question, as it presented itself to them with the memory of the previous evening still fresh in their minds. And during the day, at intervals, delegates would be seen to whisper and then chuckle, as the question was repeated again and again. But Meyer conquered the hilarity of the morning and the very laughter emphasised his appeal.

In the Metropolis, with all the zest of a new-comer, he joined the Baptist Forward Movement, and was appointed its Honorary Director. With Dr. Clifford and others, including Rev. J. E. Shepherd, the minister of John Street Chapel, an ambitious attempt, arising out of a suggestion made by the Rev. William Cuff, was made to revive the Baptist work in London The Rev. Frederick C. Spurr, who was then at Cardiff, and whose church building there had become all too small, was invited to join them, and for three years, until the Forward Movement lost its impetus, he was associated with it, afterwards becoming the Missioner of the Baptist Union itself. But the Deaconess work then begun has been continued to this day, and the Medical Mission of which Dr. Percy Lush, a member of Regent's Park Church, was the consultant, had a long and honourable career.

It is a question whether the Chairmanship of the Committee of the Baptist Missionary Society, or the Presidency of the Baptist Union, is the Blue Ribbon of the Baptist Church in Great Britain. Possibly the latter would win the vote. The Vice-President, elected by the suffrage of the assembly, becomes automatically the President of the following year, and in 1906 Mr. Meyer, as a token of the esteem and confidence of his brethren, was elected to this high position, serving as President in 1907-8.

In the Spring Session in London he chose as the subject of his Presidential Address " The Opportunity of the Church." In one passage he said, " The task before us is not an easy one, but there is less difficulty, probably, for us as Baptists than for any other branch of the Free Churches. The ordinance from which we derive our name reminds us that the disciple is not above his Lord, and that we must needs be conformed to the image of His death ; ' In these days,' said William Morris, ' ye are building a house which shall not be overthrown, and the world shall not be too great, or too little to hold it, for indeed it shall be the world itself, set free from evil-doers for friends to dwell in. Therefore there is nothing that can undo us, except our own selves, and our hearkening to soft words. So do great deeds, or repent that ever you were born.' "

In his Autumn Presidential Address at Huddersfield, entitled, " The Mid-Current," there was a succession of remarkable passages. " As we turn the pages of the Bible," he says, " we are conscious of the presence there of the Spirit of Eternity, of Timelessness and of God, which is breathing through the words. No one who has once met the breath of the glaciers can ever forget it, it is like no air beside ; and no one who has stood before the Infinite God, for even a moment, needs convincing that God has spoken. The nearer a man lives to God, the more absolutely convinced he becomes of the unrivalled authorship and supremacy of the Scripture.

" In the century just closed the danger of our churches being diverted into a back eddy was counteracted by the new interest and romance of Foreign Missions, in which we are permitted to be the pioneers. An interesting illustration of this was presented to me as I was scanning the old records of the Baptist Church at Soham. Page after page is filled with the story of a dispute respecting the moral freedom of the will—whether it is in the power of men with the common gifts of rationality to will that which is morally good and to will that which is morally evil. Mixed up with these records there are minutes of four different calls given to Brother Fuller to assume the pastorate. But when the new pastor presently accepted, there was no longer space for wrangling about the Will; because *Brother* Fuller was *Andrew* Fuller, and when *he* came he taught the church to hear the cry of a perishing world. What operated in that single instance operated throughout the whole compass of our churches.

" The Lord of the Harvest knew well what He was doing when He scattered the rarest minds of England throughout the remotest parts of the country, where men have time to think, and where in sequestered nooks the springs of natural life start rivers on their great careers.

" The Lord Chancellor uttered the exact truth when he said, on the introduction of Mr. Birrell's Bill in the House of Lords, that the question between the Church and Nonconformists is the same question in a different form that arose in the time of Cromwell and Laud.

" If any man *trust* to himself that he is Christ's, let him consider this again with himself, that as he is Christ's, so also are we. Whereinsoever any is bold (we speak foolishly) we are bold also. Are they Christians ? So are we. Are they Churchmen ? So are we. Are they ministers of Christ ? So are we : in labours as abundant ; in prisons more frequent ; in weariness and painfulness ; in watchings often ; in hunger and thirst. We are members one of another. Without us the Established Church cannot be made perfect. Surely if the bishop would think again, he would raise his manacled wrists, manacled by the control of the House of Commons, and exclaim, ' I would to God that not only I, but all my brethren in the Establishment, were both almost, and altogether such as you are, including the removal of these bonds.' "

At the end of his Presidency the Council of the Union, in presenting its report, said that his year of office had " been signalised by boundless and almost inexhaustible energy and service. The most important feature of the year has been the systematic visitation, together with the Secretary, of the Associations in every part of the United Kingdom. The most interesting part of the President's tour was perhaps the Motor-car Campaign of the summer, during which upwards of seventy meetings were held in the open air in the counties of Buckinghamshire, Bedfordshire, Cambridgeshire and Oxfordshire. The people from adjoining villages and hamlets congregated together on village greens and at cross roads to receive and hear the President of the Baptist Union."

It will be noticed that much of this visitation of the country was in the company of Dr. J. H. Shakespeare, the Secretary of the Baptist Union. A very close friendship grew up between these two men. In the library of the Church House to-day full-size portraits of the two face each other. In a letter from Durban written on July 28th, 1908, Meyer says to Shakespeare, " I do so count on the alliance between us two, that we may together do a great work for Christ and our denomination." This alliance continued in various ways.

On his return from his visit to China, referred to on a later page, he was in danger of being misled by a multitude of counsellors, had not Dr. Shakespeare, with the frankness of a true friend, written him a long letter, which, if it were not marked " confidential," would reveal both Shakespeare and Meyer as real comrades. The necessity of working from some centre was made clear to him when he might otherwise, in the years that remained to him, have been caught by contrary currents and floated about the world as a derelict, an experience not unknown to some of his contemporaries. That was one reason of his satisfaction and gratitude in the last lap of his life, in his continued association with Christ Church as Pastor Emeritus, and in having a room in the church building at his disposal where he afterwards spent some of the happiest and most restful of his days.

The immediate result of Shakespeare's intervention pointing out opportunity and duty, was that he accepted the invitation to preach at Regent's Park Chapel, and in a little while to be the pastor of the church. This is the explanation of the mystery why he returned to the church he had previously relinquished. One great argument which drew him again into the denominational fold was that his help was needed in the effort soon to be made to raise £250,000 as a Ministerial Sustentation Fund and that he was the only figure with world-wide reputation available, and his help could only be effective if he himself were pastor of a Baptist Church.

He was largely identified with the Congress of the Baptist World Alliance in Philadelphia in June, 1911, where with many Russians behind him on the platform he was acknowledged as past-master in urging the delegates to contribute to the establishment of a college in Russia. This experience stood him in good stead when he came to plead at home for the British Fund. In setting it before his own people he conceived the idea of comparing it to the work of Nehemiah in building the wall of Jerusalem, and on April 23rd, 1912, with a diagram of a bit of the wall, showing 250 stones, each representing £1,000, he made a racy speech introducing the proposal, urging all classes of persons then as in the ancient time to have a share in the work. He stood as a champion preparing for a New Crusade.

During the following year he was incessant in its advocacy, visiting all parts of the country. As typical of the meetings in other parts of the country, the description by Donald Maclean of the Glasgow gathering may be taken. When Mr. Shakespeare had spoken, " After that," said the reporter, " nothing remained to be said. The people were ready. Indeed, in mere justice, it should be said that the people

were ready long ago. It was the leaders who were lacking.
Now, however, the leader had indicated the way, and the
people impatiently waited the signal to go forward.

" Dr. Meyer recognised the fact, and, dispensing with a
speech, went straight to work. To see and hear the Doctor
on an occasion like this is like reading a chapter of one of
William de Morgan's books. There is about both something
quaint and old-fashioned, together with a gentle humour,
soothing and agreeable in the highest degree, that like a
quiet stream carries you softly on to precisely the point
where he desires to land you. To those of us who are young
he feels like our grandfather, and to the middle-aged he
feels like their children's grandfather, and the sort of grandfather, be it added, who carries candy in his pockets.

" When he rose he beamed upon us as when the sun
ariseth in his strength, and as he beamed it came to pass
that a strange illusion fell upon us, and we beheld him,
not as the King of Beggars come to empty our pockets, as
he proved to be, but as Father Christmas come to fill our
stockings. Consequently, we received him rapturously.
' I wish to make a few prudent suggestions.' There does not
appear to be anything particularly humorous about that
remark when it is written down. Yet there must have been
a cinch somewhere, for the whole gathering shook with
merriment. However, the prudent suggestions were made,
and resulted in a regiment of ushers distributing promise
forms. Then there were great borrowings of pens and
pencils and much writing and signing of names, and a little
later Dr. Meyer rose again to read out details of the first
promise form that had reached him. There was silence, and
in clear, even tones the Doctor read : ' The first donation
is one thousand pounds.' There was a moment of surprised
stillness, and then a storm of applause. After that the
atmosphere was electric. It was felt now that anything
might happen. And, as a matter of fact, things did happen.
For nearly half an hour ushers ran back and forth, the
promises were checked and passed to Dr. Meyer, and he
read on continuously, commenting here and there as he

went along, and more often on the five guineas of some
village minister than on the ' hundred ' of the business man.
For a time we kept count, but the amounts were too many
and diverse, and presently one got so used to hearing,
' Mrs. So-and-so, £50,' that it had no more effect than if it
had been fivepence. Indeed, towards the finish it took at
least £500 to raise anything like enthusiasm. One can become
accustomed, it would seem, to anything.

" However, all things have an end, and the last promise
form was at length laid face down on the heap on the table.
Then came a little time of waiting while they added up the
totals. Then a moment of breathless suspense, when
Dr. Meyer stood up again to announce the total. Slowly
and impressively he read it out, ' Thirteen thousand, three
hundred and fifty pounds.' A kind of joyous hush lay on
the assembly for a moment, and then somehow we were all
on our feet singing the only possible song, ' Praise God from
Whom all blessings flow.' "

Monday by Monday Dr. Shakespeare would send
Dr. Meyer some details of the week, and in a few hours he
would receive an article based on them for *The Baptist
Times* of that week, which regularly reproduced the picture
of Nehemiah's Wall. The freshness and piquancy of these
paragraphs were a constant surprise to Shakespeare.

On May 1st 1914, at a great meeting in Westminster
Chapel, presided over by Mr. Lloyd George, Mr. Meyer
again appealed for help, with his experience in Philadelphia
and in the provinces, an expert in the business : and at the
Thanksgiving Meeting at the Albert Hall he again spoke,
giving the modern version of the Nehemiah story.

Two days previously Mr. Shakespeare wrote a letter to
him characterised by his own great qualities :

" At the close of the campaign I want to thank you very
gratefully, very affectionately and warmly for the splendid
service you have rendered, not only to the Fund, but also to me,
and also for the way you have rendered it. I always feel about
you that you are the most generous hearted and the kindest of
men. The nobility of your spirit in everything you do makes it

a constant delight to work with you. We have had a very happy time, and now I trust that the new arrangements you are making at Regent's Park will very greatly increase your happiness and prolong your service, not only in Regent's Park but also to the churches throughout all the world. It would be a pity if the far-reaching influence you have acquired should not be used in the largest possible way.

" Yours affectionately,
" J. H. SHAKESPEARE."

To which Mr. Meyer replied the next day :

" I have read your very kind letter three times and have put it away to keep. I only keep a very few. I trust that many years of happy fellowship may lie before us. Of course, I hope to be used to the last bit of the candle, though I rather wonder how, and a little bit dread the possibilities."

In a letter to the Rev. M. E. Aubrey, the present Secretary of the Baptist Union, Dr. Meyer in apologising for his absence from Committees which as Past-President of the Union he was entitled to attend, wrote under date January 6th, 1928 :

" My loyalty to our great testimony as Baptists has never faltered. But I am obliged to conserve what strength remains to me, and therefore have dropped attendance at Councils and similar gatherings. The younger generation are doing magnificently. So I join the great cloud of witnesses and watch the cricket pitch, shouting ' Well played ' for every good stroke. I am so very proud of your own leadership. Thank God ! So please don't be disappointed if I remain as I am.

" Yours very sincerely,
" F. B. MEYER."

Deeply impressive at the Session the following year was the presentation of Dr. Meyer's portrait to the Baptist Union by Mrs. Miner in memory of her husband, Mr. Charles Albert Miner, a great friend of Dr. Meyer's. Mr. Shakespeare as representing the donor, said, " In this picture from the Hon. John Collier we have not only a fine work of art, but also a

life-like presentation to later days of one of the most notable
men of our time. But the man is so much finer than his
work. He gives even better than he prays. And so,"
turning to him he said, " Mr. Meyer, we put the portrait
in our gallery as the symbol that you belong to us. Forgive
us if, just as the world never recognises the Child in the
manger, nor perceives the Kingdom in the seed, and just as
Anglicanism had no room for Baxter or Wesley, we have not
always made the most of you. Forgive us if we have not
recognised our Thomas à Kempis or known our Francis
D'Assisi. We need your illuminating sagacity, your Gospel
loyalty, your vision of Jesus, your anointing of the Holy
Ghost."

When Mr. Meyer rose to reply the assembly rose to cheer
him, and he declared that though he might go to the ends
of the earth there would always be a mystic thread unwinding
from that portrait in the Church House which would bring
him back again.

Dr. Shakespeare has written a further estimate of his
friend : " There are half a dozen men in our generation who
amaze their contemporaries by the persistency of their toil,
and the enormous amount of work they are able to do.
To very many F. B. Meyer has become a synonym for
tireless industry. The most casual observer is able to
discover that he plays many parts, each of which would be
enough to tax the energy of an ordinary man. He is the
Pastor of a large church with great traditions ; he is the
centre and inspiration of a vast Church organisation ; an
author whose books are read and prized throughout the
world ; a member of many very important committees, in
which his presence is always a directing and controlling
force ; he has been President successively of our greatest
religious and interdenominational organisations—and for
him to be President is no sinecure, as he at once devotes an
astonishing amount of energy to the position ; he is well
known at Keswick and at Northfield ; he is a leader in
national movements, of which just now the chief is education;
one of the three Free Church ministers asked for at every

big demonstration; a Councillor of the Borough of Lambeth; a friend and helper to whom countless perplexed and distressed souls repair for guidance and help; a punctilious correspondent; last, but not least, the President of the Baptist Union, devoting every possible day to its work and interests. We may well rub our eyes in amazement at such a programme, and ask, How is all this done?

" I understand the secret of it better than I did. I have known Mr. Meyer for thirty years, but during the last few months I have learnt a great deal about him which I did not properly understand. Without any hesitation I should place first that he carries out the injunction to pray without ceasing, in the sense of prayer as dependence upon God. He is never in a hurry; he always seems to have time for some fresh task. He does one thing at once, and it has for the moment all his mind, for it is the thing which the Father has given him to do."

" The extraordinary influence of Mr. Meyer rests primarily upon his reality and sincerity," he wrote at another time. " He is what he professes to be. But after continuous intercourse with him since he became our President, I attest that he is more and better than even he appears to be. He is a citizen of heaven, but his heaven is here and now in the constant presence of Christ.

" This sweetness of disposition is united with an almost autocratic temper when he has definitely decided on the right path. He cannot be easily turned aside, and if there are defections he is quite prepared to go on alone. Yet strangely enough his humility is quite touching, and he who is cram full of fresh ideas hails an ordinary suggestion by a friend with an enthusiastic gratitude as though it were an amazing discovery. I have noticed that his relation to money is always a right one. At Westminster he has been content with a small salary, and even then has given it back again. But he knows that he must have money for all his enterprises and charities; to help young fellows at college, to support sisters and workers, and somehow the money comes to him. But all his life he has set aside a definite proportion to God.

He keeps an account with God, and therefore he always has money to give away in an emergency. Finally, he is intensely human, but he has conquered all animal passions. An early riser, temperate and simple in his manner of life, even food and sleep hold a minor place in his programme.

" His industry and vitality are amazing. Travelling often three nights a week, speaking five hours a day, then hurrying back to his church, he showed what he could do to enlarge the horizon of the church. Wherever he goes crowds gather. It is simply the extension of this service that now, liberated from the burden of his church work, he should travel as an apostle through the world, carrying with him everywhere the contagion of his personal force and imparting the vitalizing ideas, the social and religious convictions which have become the ' master light of all his seeing.'

" He has now accepted this rôle of apostle. His mission in a peculiar degree will be catholic and cosmopolitan. In a sense which, perhaps, applies to no other living man, he will have a world-wide cure of souls. Just as Paul said, ' I must see Rome also,' so Mr. Meyer has gone step by step, advancing to a fresh height of life."

CHAPTER NINE

As a Free Churchman

DR. MEYER'S sympathies, as we have seen, went out to the whole Church of Christ, but first, last, and midst, he belonged to the Free Churches. In 1904 he was President of the Free Church Council, and when disaster seemed to threaten that organisation after the tragic death of the Rev. Thomas Law, who had done so much to build it up, Dr. Meyer, with his usual knight-errantry, volunteered in 1910 to step into the breach until such time as other satisfactory arrangements could be made, little thinking that his tenure of the office would run to ten years, and that before he finished he would need to devote his whole time to it.

In the midst of Dr. Meyer's Secretariat a leading journal in reviewing the position of the Council said : " We are glad to know that the genius, hard work, and magnetic personality of Dr. F. B. Meyer have stimulated into new life many local Councils that had become nearly moribund. But we know, too, that many still remain lifeless, and that most are in danger, upon the removal of one or two persons from their locality, of lapsing into a living death. What would happen did Dr. Meyer cease to distribute driving power from the Memorial Hall we shudder to think."

He acted as Honorary Secretary all the time, and only on the appointment of Rev. Thomas Nightingale, who has proved himself the man for that hour, did he relinquish the post. Then for the second time he was elected President, and the Executive Committee commemorated his services in a fitting resolution, in which they expressed " Veneration for his character, and high appreciation of the remarkable services which he rendered to the Council, as well as to the cause of Christian religion in this country and throughout the world. The devotion and unworldliness of his nature, his fearless championship of great religious, moral and social causes, and his deep human sympathy made his services of unspeakable value to all the interests of the Kingdom of God."

More than once during these years his advocacy of Free Church principles, especially during the Education controversy, seemed likely to estrange him from some of his friends in the Establishment, though at other times, of course, standing forth as the representative of Protestant Nonconformity in England, he was drawn into closer fellowship with them. When he became a Passive Resister and appeared before the Lambeth Bench it seemed that he would be no longer welcome on the Keswick platform, and indeed he refused to take part in the Convention until he was assured by its leaders that his conscientious objections raised no barriers between him and them.

A great Free Church Demonstration to protest against the Education Act was held in Hyde Park on May 23rd, 1903. " Speeches continued for an hour and a half, then at 6.45 the resolution was put from every platform. It was carried unanimously with a mighty roar of cheers, men waving hats, umbrellas or walking sticks, and women, handkerchiefs or newspapers. The indignation raised by the Act had burst into flame. Every reference to Passive Resistance called forth the utmost enthusiasm. Dr. Clifford, Mr. Silvester Horne and Mr. Meyer were the Kings of the demonstration." A description of the scene from Mr. Meyer's platform says " He never looked more handsome than on this open-air pulpit, his grey hair fluttered by the breeze, and his pale, refined features slightly flushed by the excitement of the hour. You would scarcely choose him as a typical park orator, yet no speaker is more distinctly heard."

Prior to his official connection with the Council he had rendered important service in connection with the Simultaneous Mission the Council organised in 1901, not only in writing pamphlets to help the local councils and the missioners, but himself taking no inconsiderable part in the missions in various parts of the country as well as in the metropolis. He was himself President of the Metropolitan Free Church Council, and so was specially interested in London. In the great city Dr. Parker inaugurated the Mission by a sermon in the Guildhall, and then special meetings were held in over fifty centres of Greater London. Probably more people were reached in the aggregate than even in the great Mission conducted by Moody and Sankey in fewer centres, and the success in London greatly increased the enthusiasm in the country a fortnight later. The death of Queen Victoria on January 22nd during the progress of the London meetings gave an added solemnity to the occasion.

His Presidential Address at Newcastle in 1904 had as its topic " The Duties of the Free Churches in an Age of Reaction." After naming the reactionary forces he proceeded to speak of the duties to which the churches should address themselves—the training of the young, keeping the spiritual aspects of our work well to the front, securing a higher standard of Christian living, maintaining a closer fellowship with the Spirit of Jesus Christ and seeking a new endowment of power. " The names of our theologians and social reformers," he cried, " of our politicians and philanthropists, shine as brightly and numerously as any in our national roll-call. Our Moffats and Livingstones, our Spurgeons and Dales, our Parkers and Punshons, our Samuel Morleys and Cadburys, our Maclarens and Cliffords, men like the late lamented Charles Berry and Hugh Price Hughes, will rank amongst the foremost of their age in their contribution to the making of modern England."

In 1920 the subject of the Presidential address at Leicester was " The Fellowship of the Free Churches," in which he urged the consecration by the churches of The Universal Craving for Amusement, the Soul's instinctive challenge to High-handed Wrong, the Natural Tendency towards Comradeship and the Sacred Institution of the

Home. Great interest was aroused by one item on the programme : " Methods, Means and Mastery—Surprise Address by the President," which resolved itself into a most successful appeal for money, Dr. Meyer using to the full the experience he had gained at the Baptist World Congress in America, and in the Baptist Sustentation appeal in Westminster Chapel.

In his frequent journeys on the business of the Council he often had the companionship of Mr. G. H. Saunders, the Editor of *The Free Churchman*, who has been good enough to recall some most interesting mutual experiences.

" At one time I was associated with Dr. Meyer in an affair that called for considerable business acumen. For hours he was in committee with well-known men, directors of companies, accountants, lawyers and others, and throughout the proceedings he showed a masterly grip of details. After the meeting I remarked to him that some of those who knew him as a saintly preacher only, would be astonished to know that he could hold his own when intricate matters of business were under discussion. ' Well, you see,' explained Dr. Meyer, ' I have inherited a dual personality. I come from a long line of successful business men on my father's side, and my mother was a very saintly woman. My mother's influence predominated, but I know my father gave me a keen sense of business.'

" One of Dr. Meyer's outstanding characteristics was his remarkable powers of concentration. Conditions that would be distracting to others he found congenial. He found the train, for instance, an ideal place in which to work. If he had a long journey before him he would settle himself in his corner of the railway carriage with a sigh of relief, open his despatch case, which was fitted up as a sort of stationery cabinet, and set to work in supreme contentment on some abstruse article, quite oblivious of his surroundings. Often at protracted conventions and even in committee meetings, when the proceedings did not demand his undivided attention, he would unobtrusively open his case and proceed to answer letters.

" Dr. Meyer was the personification of charity. He could never resist the appeal of any one who was down and out and consequently he was often the victim of the ' sponger.' He was well aware of this, but he often said that ' it was far better to be let down occasionally than never to have the satisfaction of lending a helping hand.' He believed that he was merely a trustee of the Lord in money matters. To him money was simply the means whereby he could help his fellow men. With his amazing literary and oratorical gifts he could easily have amassed a fortune, but he was careless of his own financial position. Sufficient unto him was the knowledge that he was doing the Lord's will. If money came to him as a result of his efforts, well and good. If it did not he was still satisfied. He had the simple abiding trust that his Heavenly Father would provide for his needs, and for the work he was called upon to do.

" Often he would find himself without a penny in his pocket but this never troubled him. Sometimes he would go to a station far away in the country to get his return ticket and then would discover that he had no money with him. In such a case he would go straight to the station-master and explain his position, and so well-known and respected was he that never on any occasion when he was in such a predicament did a servant of the railway company fail him.

" Owing to his generosity it was a common thing for Dr. Meyer to be temporarily hard up, but this never upset him in the slightest. ' It is the Lord's work,' he would say, ' and He will provide.' And strange as it may appear to some, the Lord always did provide in some mysterious way.

" I remember on one occasion a man came to see him at the Memorial Hall. He was only slightly known to the Doctor, but he told such a pitiful tale of misery and bad fortune that he felt moved to help him. The man said that a great opportunity had come to him to take a share in a fried fish shop, but he needed the sum of five pounds. Dr. Meyer went thoroughly into the story and

eventually, being satisfied as to the truth of it, handed over
the money—all that he had upon him at the moment.

"When I saw him later he asked me if I had any
money I could lend him. It so happened that I had only a
shilling or two at the moment and by a strange coincidence
there was no money available in the office just then.

"'Never mind,' said Dr. Meyer, cheerfully. 'I've got
to start for the North in a few minutes, and my ticket will
cost three pounds. It is God's business and He will see to
it.' And without another thought he dismissed the matter
from his mind.

"Shortly after he began to open his private correspondence. The very first letter he picked up contained
five one pound notes! 'There,' exclaimed Dr. Meyer,
triumphantly, 'I said the Lord would provide!' Of course
the money in the letter was in payment of some services he
had rendered, and one might say that it was only coincidence
that it should arrive at such an opportune moment; but
the fact remains that such 'coincidences' were always
happening and were an everyday occurrence.

"As a matter of fact he rejoiced in such occurrences,
and in his simple way would accept them as direct answers
to prayer. At one time he was due to preach at
Hitchin. As usual, anxious to make the best use of his
time, he had hung on at the office until the very last
moment, and he was only just able to tumble into a carriage
as the train was on the move. He collected himself and
settled down to his correspondence, when he began to wonder
if he was in the right train! He sought the guard, who told
him that the train went straight through to Peterborough
and did not stop at Hitchin. Here was a predicament! He
had barely allowed himself sufficient time to keep his
preaching appointment, and now he would soon be flying
through the town.

"'Well,' said Dr. Meyer in relating the incident, 'I just
went down on my knees in that railway carriage and told
the Lord all about it and threw the burden upon Him and
went on with my work. Soon the train approached Hitchin,

and to my astonishment and joy we began to slow down. We were almost at a standstill as we reached the station, and seizing the opportunity I opened the door and jumped out, just as the train began to gather speed again.'

" A trivial incident in itself maybe, but such incidents, multiplied many times over as they were in his life, assume an importance that cannot be carried by the word " coincidences."

" Though he was such a prodigious worker himself, he was full of consideration for others and never expected that they should equal his own efforts. At one time there was a convention at Scarborough. I, a young man at the time, travelled up North very comfortably the day before. Dr. Meyer on the other hand had had a very hard day and found it necessary to travel all through the night to be in time for the Scarborough meetings. As usual, he was the life and soul of the gatherings, of which there were half a dozen, and which did not end until nearly ten o'clock.

" I walked with him to the station, where we had to wait some time for the London train, as he had to be at the office early the next day for an important engagement. When we were on the platform Dr. Meyer said to me : ' My dear man, you must not wait any longer, you've had a long day. Get back and have a good night's rest.' ' That's all very well,' I replied. ' But what about you ? You've had a far heavier time than I, and you look like having very little sleep in any case.' ' That's all right,' he said, with that humorous twinkle that came so readily to his eye, ' but we needn't both be fools. I don't want you to get into the silly habit of burning the candle at both ends.'

" Though it was an almost everyday occurrence for Dr. Meyer to spend nights in the train, this habit did not adversely affect him, for he had a wonderful facility for sleep. The power of concentration which he brought to bear upon his work he could also direct upon himself, so that he could almost in any place and in any circumstances sink into slumber, to awake from it shortly afterwards, thoroughly refreshed. I have known him in the midst of his work to relax himself and snatch a few minutes' sleep and then proceed with his work with renewed vigour. He would sleep in the train, in the taxicab and in the omnibus, and I have even known him to snatch ' forty winks ' during an exceptionally long-drawn committee."

A great feature of his year of office was the motor tours which, in company with other Free Church leaders, he undertook in all parts of the country, the object being to reach the more inaccessible small towns and villages. He had already had experience in this kind of propaganda during the Education Controversy, and he always amazed his companions by his capacity for work. However tired he may have appeared in the morning, he became fresher and fresher as the day wore on. Dr. Charles Brown describes two of these motor tours in North Wales. After praising the scenery and expressing gratitude for the great number of people, often at inconvenient hours, to greet them, he says :

" Perhaps the most outstanding impression left on one's mind from these two Welsh tours is the amazing versatility of Dr. Meyer, and his unconventionality. He is equal to any situation, from making tea in a cottage kitchen, when the motor car has broken down, to solemnly exhorting a company of learned ministers. The only situation to which he is not equal is that in which every moment is not crowded with work. The only day when I saw him distressed was a day in which we had only five meetings, and there was half an hour when we could neither journey nor address people. Wherever possible he was keen on having our meeting in the open air, so we would bring people out of the chapel into the market-place, and there with hundreds of people around we would explain what a Free Church and a Free Church Council is, and our dear friend would pour out his heart in a fervent evangelistic appeal.

" It would have greatly impressed some of our people to have seen Dr. Meyer and myself, as in the little town of Montgomery, standing in the open square, and shouting to the houses which looked as if they were asleep, that we had come from London, and were going to hold a meeting in the chapel, and we hoped everybody would come and hear what we had to say : then leading a procession through the startled streets, singing ' Guide me, O Thou great Jehovah,' to a Welsh tune, and so getting all sorts of people into the chapel. Once during our two tours we were moved on by the police just as I had begun to speak, and once we were refused permission to hold a meeting. For the rest we went on unhindered.

" They were wonderful days, full of happy fellowship, of inspiring services, and of divine blessing. We are quite certain from all we saw and heard that the visits will result in the quickening and strengthening of the life and faith of the churches with whose representatives we met. Our meetings were by no means on a dead level of uniformity. One may express the firm and reverent conviction that we were led of the Spirit in our methods and addresses."

The Annual Report of the Council for 1905 said quite candidly that the visitation of the country was in its thoroughness an example " of the extraordinary thoroughness characteristic of the man." A number of testimonies are also given from many quarters. " If it was evident that the candle of the Lord was in the hand of the speaker, it was no less certain that the speaking was in demonstration of the Spirit and in power."

In September, 1907, Mr. Meyer, having resigned the pastorate of Christ Church, began, in connection with the Free Church Council, a Mission campaign in various parts of England, and after six months representing the Council, journeyed to South Africa, where he had a triumphant welcome, to which reference will be made in a later chapter. Then as we have seen he became Honorary Secretary for ten years, and in resigning that post he said " that as his life was coming to its consummation he desired to light fires all through the world that would burn when he was gone "—a desire very largely fulfilled during the next, the last, decade of his eventful life.

" In the first period of my life," he said, " I trusted Christ for short trips, and He never failed me. Since then I have trusted Him for longer and longer journeys, along unknown roads, and still He has never failed me, so that I now believe He knows all the roads."

At the end of his second term of Presidency he wrote : " The unveiling of the Cenotaph and the opportunity afforded of representing the Free Churches both there and at the Abbey : the memorable Mayflower Celebrations in Holland, Plymouth and elsewhere : the negotiations with the Archbishop and Bishops arising out of the Lambeth proposals—these have been occasions of unusual importance. Our Free Church Council movement has been enhanced in value and service, and we are realising the importance of this valuable organisation, which expresses the consensus and virility of our corporate life."

" The Free Churches elected Dr. Meyer to every office in which it was in their power to place him, and every position he filled he adorned," says Mr. D. J. Findlay of Glasgow. " It is not so well known—because his modesty kept him from telling such matters—that again and again in national crises Dr. Meyer was sent for by those in highest position to give his valued counsel and help : and not once or twice he was able to give such help as proved to be of priceless value."

He preserved a sheaf of letters from eminent persons— archbishops, bishops, preachers, statesmen and authors. With some hesitation one from our present Prime Minister, written just after his wife's death, may be transcribed.

" 3, Lincoln's Inn Fields, W.C.,

" 13th September, 1911.

" MY DEAR MR. MEYER,

" I want to thank you for coming yesterday and bringing peace and comfort with you. My children have now gone for the time being and I am alone with her in my heart. In a few days I shall get away too, and shall try to get back to the ploughing and sowing again as she would wish.

" Yours always gratefully and sincerely,

" J. RAMSAY MACDONALD."

CHAPTER TEN

THE BROTHERHOOD

THE problem that awaited Mr. Meyer when he went to
Christ Church was the reverse of that which presented itself
to him in Leicester and at Regent's Park. In these places
his church was amongst people of the social order who
generally attend Christian worship, and it was necessary to
search for the degraded and careless folk. Christ Church,
on the contrary, borders on the slums, if it is not actually
in the midst of them, and it was necessary to attract the
more reputable strata of society to the neighbourhood.
There was also the difficulty that the building seemed over-
whelmingly grand to those who lived in tenements, and
almost repellent to the abject poor.

" I was encountered with most gloomy prognostications,"
he wrote, " of the result of my endeavour to make Christ
Church the home of the working people that throng the
adjacent streets. ' It can't be done,' said the prophets.
' In the old days the working classes would throng Surrey
Chapel on a Monday for a Popular Lecture : but this place
is too imposing, too ecclesiastical, too much associated with
top hats and kid gloves. It is the church of the better classes.
You will never be able to blend the two.' And they pointed
me to the scanty handful of men and women that composed
the afternoon Mission Service, as a beacon to warn me off
the rocks of failure."

" On the other hand, one afternoon before I entered
upon my new charge, whilst walking over Westminster
Bridge towards Christ Church, it was definitely impressed
upon me that I was to undertake a Sunday Afternoon

Meeting for men. This, therefore, made me strong against all argument and recapitulation of past failure."

It was in the days when P.S.A.'s were flourishing, and though a great deal was accomplished by their means, their success was only partial and scarcely permanent, while the idea underlying the title, that only something pleasant would attract men, and the half-hint that the other services of the churches were not pleasant, made it desirable that something different should be attempted.

My friend the Rev. J. K. Nuttall, of George Street Chapel, Liverpool, the minister of a great church in the heart of the city, hit upon the idea of a " Brotherhood," and gathered a great crowd of men from all over Liverpool to his church on Sunday afternoons. The success achieved in the city where he himself had begun his ministry, and the method by which it was obtained, appealed strongly to Mr. Meyer ; he approved the plan, and, with his usual skill, improved upon it. A Brotherhood it should be, the members should call each other " Brother," and while always maintaining a high aim, the social instincts of the men should have fair consideration. Of course, such an effort needed a great deal of preparation. Prejudice had to be overcome, expectancy aroused, curiosity excited, and those who knew how to pray had to be summoned to earnest intercession.

The first Sunday in December, 1893, saw the launching of the project, and at first it seemed as if everything went wrong ; the appointed singer failed, and the men came in but slowly ; but before the time announced some two hundred men turned up, and at the meeting sixty gave their names for permanent attendance. The ice thawed, the idea grew from less to more, the men actually applauded the speakers, and before long they felt the meeting was their own. After a while it was no uncommon thing to see the area of the church crowded with interested and eager attendants.

At first they spoke of their leader as one of themselves : he was " Brother Meyer." But before long they found a new name for him. I quote his own account of how it came about. " The following is a reminiscence of an address given by my friend Mr. Fullerton one Sunday afternoon, and its results. ' There was an old tug which ran between London and Portsmouth,' he said, ' a queer-shaped, ugly old craft, more like a badly-built tub than a boat, and her name painted on her bow was—well, I'll not tell you that, but she was nicknamed " Old-Bust-'em-up " ; for whenever she came into dock she always collided with some vessel, and did it some damage, or by bumping against a vessel injured herself. If by any chance she managed to get clear of the craft when coming into dock, she was bound to damage either the dock-gates or herself, so clumsily handled was she. But one day to the wonderment of all who were gathered on the shore, " Old-Bust-'em-up " was seen coming in as straight as a die, keeping clear of all vessels. She seemed to glide like a swan to her place in the dock. An old salt who stood by could not hold his peace when he saw this, and shouted " What ho ! ' Old Bust-'em-up,' what's the matter with you ? " Back from the boat there came the reply, " The same old boat, guv'nor, but we've got a new Skipper on board."

" ' Ah, man,' said Mr. Fullerton "—and I am still quoting from *Reveries and Realities*—" ' You may have been an old " Bust-'em-up " yourself, damaging yourself and others in your life's journey ; but if you will take the new Skipper— the Lord Jesus Christ—on board, and let Him pilot your life, you shall sail perfectly straight henceforth.'

" In that audience was a man who had just come out of jail for drunkenness and other offences : and as he said afterwards, he ' sat and listened and drank it all in.' He had damaged, almost blasted, his own life, besides being guilty of damaging the lives of others. It seemed as if the devil had taken possession of him, but the man took the new Skipper aboard that afternoon, and ever since he did that, he has been a different man.

" The story of this man's conversion was told to me by the missionary of the police court where he had been convicted. The missionary had been trying hard to get the

man to decide for Christ, but up till then the services of
the new Skipper had been refused. But now, thanks be to
God ! he is humbly rejoicing in his newly-found Saviour,
and his happy restoration to his wife and children.   In
addition to this an old employer promised to give him work :
and this man is now working at his old trade under him."

This is only a sample of many others who were arrested
and reclaimed at this meeting. It is recounted, not only for
its own interest, but for the suggestion it gave to the
members of the meeting as to their leader. They recognised
the meaning of the name as it had first been applied, but a
genius among them did not see why another use should not
be made of it, and from that day they called Mr. Meyer
" The Skipper." He took kindly to it, and considering what
he had been able to do in guiding their lives into safe courses
it appeared to be most apposite ; and to have earned a
nickname was a sure guarantee of achieved success.

Rev. F. A. Robinson of Toronto tells in *The Sunday
School Times*, how one day " As we were leaving one of
Ontario's most beautiful churches at the close of an afternoon's service, a very dirty hand was suddenly thrust
towards Dr. Meyer as he settled down in a luxurious car.
' Hello, Skipper,' said a rough-looking chap. How radiantly
surprised the aged preacher was. ' Skipper ! ' What
memories the word revived ! It was in Lambeth, the most
densely populated district of old London : Lambeth, with
its tenements and filthy lodging-houses, with its sin and
shame and poverty, that he had received that title. The
men ' down at the heel,' the homeless, hopeless, lonely,
despairing men had called him that. They went to him
because they had a burden or needed guidance, and the
' Skipper ' never failed them.

" ' I can't tell you how my heart was thrilled by that
word " Skipper ",' he told the audience that night. ' How
I want to thank that dear man for calling me that in the
midst of these respectable people ! Oh, how I wish I could
still do that work ! Those crowds of rough working men, and
drunkards, and men sick of life ! I had eight hundred of them

every Sunday afternoon, and, mind you, I never talked politics or economics, but always Jesus Christ, and there were conversions by the scores.' "

For the dual service at the church, Mr. Meyer seemed almost to possess a dual personality. On Sunday mornings and evenings, when he attracted a great congregation, he was the ecclesiastic, growing each year more ethereal and refined, until he bore a curious resemblance to Cardinal Manning. There was a dignity and austerity in his bearing that marked him as a saint if not as an ascetic, and he was spoken of in some circles as the Father Faber of the Free Churches. But in the afternoons with his men he delighted just to be " The Skipper," bluff and cheerful, giving orders, of course, and expecting them to be obeyed, challenging the best in the men and in the meeting, and guiding it with consummate skill.

There were two corners in the church named respectively Teetotal Corner and Consecration Corner, the first for those who wished to sign the pledge, the second for those who wished to help or desired to become Christians. Of course, there was soon a meeting for women on Monday, and a fine rivalry between the two, and all sorts of necessary clubs and societies, a bank, a prize choir and no end of committees all hard at work contributing to the success of Brotherhood and the Women's "At Home."

" In my judgment," wrote the Skipper, " nothing has happened of more interest than this incident. One of the ladies of the church, the wife of a leading official, who up to then had not seen it to be her duty to be a professed total abstainer, was visiting a poor woman in this district, discovered that her snare was intemperance, and urged her to sign the pledge. She was startled by the enquiry whether she herself was a teetotaller, and had to reply in the negative, and to her surprise the woman challenged her by saying ' I will sign the pledge if you will.'

" My friend had no alternative but to assent. On her arrival home she told her husband what had happened, a little wondering what he would think of her action. He,

however, told her that he would do the same. When
I heard of this resolve on the part of my friend and his wife,
I said that, as Samson refused to die unless he could cause
the death of as many as possible, so it would be a mistake
for them to sign the pledge without securing the adhesion
of at least twenty men and women for the same good cause."

He challenged the Brotherhood on Sunday afternoon,
and succeeded in getting twenty responses : but the greatest
excitement was to perform a similar attempt with the
women on the Monday afternoon.

"When my friend's wife told her story, I rose, and
informed the women that we must have twenty signatories
to the pledge before the meeting closed : but that we would
have a cup of strong tea first to prepare us for the effort.
After tea I stood on the platform to count the hands, as one
after another they were uplifted. Without much difficulty
we reached ten : then came a pause : then another hand
uplifted, and another : and rather slowly, another : then a
long break. If there had been difficulty in getting twenty
men out of 800, how much more difficulty would there be in
obtaining twenty women out of 250, of which 130 were
already pledged. The tension of expectation was pretty
severe : I kept encouraging the faltering resolutions as well
as I could. Presently two or three hands were uplifted in
succession, and finally we reached the total of twenty-one
who, for the first time, were prepared to sign the pledge.

"The women were highly delighted. They laughed
and clapped, and presently rose to sing ' Praise God from
Whom all blessings flow.' And now, as the result of that
visit to save a fallen sister, some hundred men and women
have put their hands to the pledge, which is in so many
cases a stepping-stone to the reception of Jesus Christ."

With such achievements to his credit Mr. Meyer became
a recognised leader in the Brotherhood Movement, was
elected President of the National P.S.A. Brotherhood Council
for the year 1906, and President of the London Federation
in 1911, when his address was on " Brotherhood : the
Mighty Solvent." He visited many parts of the country

in the interests of the Movement, initiating similar efforts, and, in giving the guidance of his experience gleaning further, hints for his own meetings. His avocation helped his vocation. He had learnt the lesson which so many miss, which some spend a lifetime in learning, that the best way to multiply is to divide. As he gave he gained ; spending early and late he did not lay waste his powers, he increased them, and that because he was living in the spiritual realm all the while.

At the Liverpool Brotherhood Conference, the afternoon proceedings were of an unusually interesting character. The roll-call of the divisional federations were accompanied by a motto, given to each division by Mr. Meyer.

The men of Scotland were told to " Soften your hearts and harden your heads." The men of Lancashire were exhorted to " Spin strong and weave close." To the men of Yorkshire the message was given, " Be as great as you are big." To the delegates from the Eastern Counties the exhortation was given, " Carry the morning in your faces." The London contingent was told, " Go back and build a New Jerusalem beside the banks of Father Thames." Those from the west of England were given the motto, " Fight the devil as your fathers fought the Spaniards and the Pope."

On St. Bartholomew's Day, August 24th, 1912, the 250th Anniversary of the Great Ejectment, Commemoration celebrations were held, in which Mr. Meyer took a conspicuous part, marching at the head of a procession from the Memorial Hall, Farringdon Street, where the meeting was held, to the Martyrs' Memorial in Smithfield, where again there was another service, and still a further meeting in the evening. A striking feature of the occasion was the presence of more than fifty ministers of churches in various parts of the country whose churches dated from 1662.

The great events of the year of Dr. Meyer's Presidency of the London Federation were the meeting at Bishopsgate Institute when he was installed, and the great demonstration at the Albert Hall, both held on a Saturday evening. On the first occasion Mr H. Jeffs, the Editor of the *Christian*

World Pulpit, the retiring President, said " My star, which is one of the seventh magnitude, is to pale its light before a star of the ' first magnitude '." There was great cheering when Mr. Meyer enumerated the two great rules of Brotherhoods—the least possible for self, and the most possible for others.

At the Albert Hall Dr. Meyer began his address with the words " Sisters and Brothers," and most of the other speakers followed his example. He reminded the great meeting that the P.S.A. of former years threatened to be a Sunday afternoon entertainment, but it had then become the virile Brotherhood of Sunday afternoon, and was succeeded by the sweet and beautiful Sisterhood of Monday afternoon and evening : indeed, he said that in some parts of the country Monday was looked upon as the women's evening out, while the men take their shift with the kids : on which, of course, there was a good deal of laughter.

His friend the Rev. James Mursell, once after a meeting of a highly intense devotional nature, accompanied him to a service in a working class neighbourhood, heard from him an address of the plainest and most practical character, and expressed his surprise that in the same day, almost in the same breath, he was able to speak in both strains. " Oh," said Meyer, " I speak off different layers, a deeper layer for the more deeply taught, one nearer the surface for plainer folk like those to-night." It was just an example of the manifoldness of the man.

To Mr. Mursell he addressed the two following letters which, with advantage, may find a place here :

" Regent's Park Chapel,

February 5th, 1912.

" MY VERY DEAR FRIEND,

" . . . I spend a good deal of time at the Memorial Hall, directing the work of F.C.C., and my Church undeniably suffers. But I love to have a church and do the best I can for my poor people. When the right man appears for the F.C.C. I will thankfully resign it, and resume the work of preaching which I love best and for which I am most suited by temperament and gifts.

" They say that I have saved the F.C.C. by God's blessing, and the position of Honorary Secretary has given me a considerable voice in public affairs. But our national life is deteriorating and it is miserable business to be always protesting and warning. After all, the constructive work is best, and one breath from God would alter in a moment the entire outlook. I have had to protest against the indecencies of the stage and the practice of Sunday shooting, which don't make me a *persona grata*. But what does it matter ?

" Your loving friend,

" F. B. MEYER."

" Christ Church,

" *June* 19*th*, 1903.

" MY DEAR MURSELL,

" I am so thankful that God has given me this opportunity of being true to my deepest convictions. What a terrible thing it would have been if I was known only as one who stood well with everybody, but whose convictions were merged like rocks under the waves. It is a matter of hourly gratitude that I have been permitted to take my stand with the Nonconformists of every age in protest against wrong.

" I think that my pleasant connection with the Established Church rested on the assumption on their part that I had sunk my destructive convictions, and they presumed, perhaps, that I had no backbone ; this, however, thank God, is put right, and men know me as I am, and always have been, in my heart of hearts.

" There is nothing you can do, except pray for me and leave the result. Our lot has fallen in very difficult times, but I do hope we may play the men for God and our country.

" Yours affectionately,

" F. B. MEYER."

During the Dock Strike Mr. Meyer visited one of Rev. J. C. Carlile's church services at Bermondsey on a Wednesday evening. A large number of dock labourers were present, many of them very tired by their long march through the streets of London, and very hungry with no prospect of a meal. He gave one of his finest addresses, full of spiritual insight, talked for nearly forty minutes on " The Trials and the Faith of Abraham," and closed with a beautiful prayer for the wives and the children. After the Benediction, when he said " Amen," there was an outburst of loud applause. The men clapped their hands and shuffled their feet, while many called " 'Core, 'core." One of the dockers stood up and said, " Won't the Reverend do another turn ? " Mr. Meyer was obviously taken aback, but he gave an encore, and talked about the deeper things. Instead of the meeting finishing at nine it closed at nearly eleven, and then a few men stayed for a personal talk and prayer.

Out of the Brotherhood grew efforts to help boys and girls, and in a street opposite the church Mr. Meyer again became the proprieter of a coffee shop and club house, where the men could gather for games and social intercourse. " A practical mystic," like Cromwell, he carried the consciousness of God with him everywhere, and as he grew older he became even more ready for lowly service. " Why," he would say, on occasion, " I am just God's errand boy."

CHAPTER ELEVEN

As Telemachus

A ROMANTIC INTERLUDE

WHEN he spoke on one occasion in the Birmingham Town Hall Dr. Meyer wondered whether he would be better known in the future as the Architect of Nehemiah's Wall or as the man who stopped a Prize Fight. He would, of course, have been the first to acknowledge that he did neither alone, but he was recognised in both, and yet his fame does not depend on the one or on the other, though he was very active and daring in both, and in each worthy of honour. Reference has already been made to one of these exploits, and this chapter will be concerned with the other.

Though he himself was a man of peace and in no sense a muscular saint, it was not such an unexpected thing as it seemed for him to interfere in a fight. In his Leicester days, one Sunday morning after the service in his church at Melbourne Hall, he was on his way home when he was attracted by a crowd who were gathered round a band of ruffians who were attacking some Salvationists. Heedless of the risk, he made his way at once between the ringleader of the mob and the Captain of the Army, and said, " I will give you permission to strike me, but you must not touch these officers : and though I have to preach again this evening, I will not leave this spot until you leave them alone and go away." His boldness prevailed, the bullies slunk away, the crowd dispersed rather ashamed of itself, and the Salvation lassies were saved from further molestation at the moment, while the incident had no little effect in preventing in the future a treatment which till then had been of quite usual occurrence.

117

It was while he was Secretary of the Free Church
Council and so far occupied a position of leadership, that
he interfered in a prize fight, the announcement of which
aroused a good deal of curiosity and excitement and abhor-
rence.   An American negro pugilist, Jack Johnson, was
matched to fight a white man, Bombardier Wells, at Earl's
Court, London, on October 2nd, 1911, and feeling ran so
high that, whichever won, it was probable that relations
would be strained not only between Britain and the United
States, but between the black race and the white.   Meyer
determined to interfere, and to prevent the fight if possible.
What searchings of heart led up to his decision can only
be guessed, but once his decision was taken he lost no
moment and missed no opportunity in bringing the influence
of decent people to oppose the encounter.

There is, of course, an element of exaggeration in comparing him to the ancient monk, but the Rev. Samuel
Chadwick in *Joyful News*, at the time made no apology for
styling him " A Modern Telemachus," and the suggestion,
even after the lapse of years, may still be accepted.

It will not be amiss to outline the classic story, before
recounting the modern parallel.   The Roman Empire had
long declared itself Christian, but in the Coliseum at Rome
the gladiatorial contests still continued.   In the year 408,
on December 24th (the time of the old Saturnalia, which
had been consecrated as the festival of the birth of Christ,
but still carried with it much of its pagan flavour), a Christian,
Alypius, taunted as a Galilean because of his unwillingness
to join them, was dragged by a group of young men to the
scene of the encounter.   His friend Telemachus, a youthful
monk, followed them and at last managed to whisper to
Alypius, " Stand firm, O my brother," and to get his
answer, " Fear me not, Telemachus, they may drag me into
this temple of Satan, but they cannot make me look on
their sacrifice of blood.   Never again will I lend my voice
to swell the demon shout over deeds of murder."

With shut eyes he sat during one combat, nor did he
open them when the crowd hailed the conqueror.   But

when two other famous gladiators appeared, and the fight became fiercer, the cries more insistent, the frenzy of the spectators more intense, the old instincts revived, the blood coursed hot and fierce through his veins, and throwing away his christian vows as he cast off his garment, he started to his feet and joined in the yells and cheers.

Telemachus too had risen to his feet, looking towards Alypius with anguish and horror. " O Christ, strengthen me ! " he cried, and before any one could stop him he was in the arena, between the gladiators, reminding them of Him who came, as on that night, to make men brothers. The gladiators stood with lowered swords, uncertain what to do, but the infuriated people, baulked of their spectacle, cried in fury that the monk should be flung to the lions, and a crowd rushed upon him, leaving him bruised and torn between the two gladiators. Then a sudden awe fell on the spectators : without a word they began to steal from their seats, while in the empty amphitheatre Telemachus lay, with his head on the knee of the repentant Alypius, until a radiance as from heaven came across his face and he pressed the hand of his friend saying : " It is peace, O my brother ! Peace on earth, good will to men. Glory ! " And so he passed —passed from the Coliseum which, because of his deed, was never afterwards wet with human blood.

No doubt it is extravagant to compare the two peace-makers, and yet Meyer influenced more people by his act than Telemachus. Though he did not give his life he faced a very fierce opposition ; the Sunday when the decision hung in the balance a rowdy crowd besieged Regent's Park Chapel. And the mere outlay in money in conducting the agitation which led to the victory was in itself very considerable.

There was a very real peril in the situation, for when the negro pugilist fought at Reno in Nevada in July of that year, serious threats were made that if he won he would be shot : as a precaution suspected people were put into jail in such numbers that the jails could hold no more, and fire-arms were impounded. Thousands of negroes in other big cities of America were beaten and mobbed, some were even killed, because they had shouted for Johnson. So there was abundant justification for stopping the fight that was planned for London.   The question was, who should take the lead ?

Here, Thomas Carlyle's paragraph about John Sterling must be quoted, because it might almost have been written about F. B. Meyer.   Julius Hare was Sterling's tutor at Trinity College, Cambridge, and " he celebrated the wonderful and beautiful gifts, the sparkling ingenuity, ready logic, eloquent utterance, and noble generosities and pieties of his pupil : records in particular how once, on a sudden alarm of fire in some neighbouring College edifice while his lecture was proceeding, all hands rushed out to help ; how the undergraduates instantly formed themselves in lines from the fire to the river, and in swift continuance kept passing buckets as was needful, till the evening was fast yielding— when Mr. Hare, going along the line was astonished to find Sterling at the river-end of it, standing up to his waist in water, deftly dealing with the buckets as they came and went. ' You in the river, Sterling : you with your coughs and dangerous tendencies of health ! '—' Somebody must be in it,' answered Sterling, ' why not I as well as another ? ' ' "

On which Carlyle remarks that " Sterling's friends "— and we may remark that Meyer's friends—" may remember many traits of that kind. The swiftest in all things, he was apt to be found at the head of the column, whithersoever the march might be ; if towards any brunt of danger, there was he surest to be at the head ; and of himself and his peculiar risks and impediments he was negligent at all times, even to an excessive and plainly unreasonable degree."

In taking his place as Secretary at the head of the agitation he used all the machinery of the Free Church Council, gained the support of the Chairman of the London County Council, which had given the license for the contest ; secured the adherence of a prominent sporting peer to support the protest for racial reasons ; and induced the Bishop of London to join this peer in sending out a memorial for signature to be submitted to the Home Secretary.

Resolutions poured into Mr. Meyer's room in shoals (on one morning there were no fewer than 260), and at length the Home Secretary declared that what was contemplated was illegal, and in spite of the fact that thirty-eight clergymen had booked seats for the occasion, the fight was abandoned.

The result was greeted with indignation on one side, and with rejoicing on the other. It was not only the churches that had opposed the fight, the average conscience of the British people was also aroused. Mr. Meyer made it clear that there was no opposition to boxing as a recreation, but only to the brutalities associated with what is known as the knock-out blow, and to the difference of races in the fight. It is not too much to say that at a bound Dr. Meyer became world-famous. The Press of all countries chronicled the victory gained for decency and good behaviour. *The Times* had two articles on the subject, and ever afterwards gave Meyer large type when he wrote to the paper, and the leading London daily papers had pages about it. A Scotch newspaper published a cartoon showing the parson knocking out both combatants, with the inscription beneath, " And I broke the jaws of the wicked, and plucked the spoil out of his teeth (The Book of Job xxix. 17)."

One of the best known London journals, having a weekly circulation of a million copies, in a page full of malice, denounced the leader of the agitation as " Meddling, Maudlin Meyer." A leading American journal wrote, " Jack Johnson's tribute to the power of the ' preachers ' marks a step forward in militant Christianity. ' They have put the front-rank fighters out of business,' he says." In view of more recent events he perhaps overstated the case. The bare statement of the result runs, " Mr. Justice Lush granted an injunction against the lessees of Earl's Court, and on Thursday the two boxers and promoters of the fight gave undertakings in the police court, to which they had been summoned on a charge of contemplating a breach of the peace, that they would not persist with the combat. The promoters of the combat undertook not to promote any contest between Johnson and Wells at any place within the

British Islands. Johnson undertook not to box with Wells anywhere within the British Empire. Some idea was entertained of transferring the combat to Paris, but Johnson announced his retirement from the ring after fulfilling his music hall engagements."

Quite justly an English journal said " The credit for frustrating the Johnson - Wells fight is due to the Rev. F. B. Meyer, who, as Secretary of the National Free Church Council, mobilised the Christian forces of the country against the combat, and took active steps to make the opposition effective." Silvester Horne in introducing him afterwards to a Brotherhood meeting at Whitefields, spoke of him as " that illustrious prizefighter." " One consequence of the protest against the Johnson-Wells contest is an outburst of popular disgust in America against the savage prize-fights under the guise of boxing matches which have been taking place in Madison Square Garden. The license of the club which promoted the fights has been forfeited. The South African press indicate great satisfaction in that Dominion at the frustration of the combat."

In jubilant mood Dr. Meyer sent a letter to the magazine *M.A.P.* in which he addressed Jack Johnson in answer to some remarks he had made.

" DEAR SIR,

" Although I quite expected that you would be vexed with me for starting an agitation which has resulted in your losing thousands of pounds, I certainly did not think that you would revenge yourself upon me in such a mean way as to refer to me as ' Bishop Meyer ' in public.

" Really, really, after a life-time devoted to the Free Church it is very hard to find myself dubbed a bishop. Numbers of papers have published your words, and as there are still a few people in the British Isles so ignorant as never to have heard of me, when they read the press reports of your remarks they will naturally conclude that I am an Anglican.

" Had you called me by even the choicest term of the boxing ring I should have forgiven you, but a bishop !

" Yours, etc.,

" F. B. MEYER."

On the merits of the case the concluding paragraphs of a long article in the London *Daily Chronicle*, by Richard Whiteing, entitled " Why Prize-Fighting is the Perfection of Hypocrisy," may be reproduced. After describing what fighting meant without gloves, he wrote :

" This was the noble art as it was until it sputtered out of existence under the extinguisher of sheer public disgust. The public would endure it no longer in that form. But the noble arters, however, were by no means at the end of their resources. The law would hear nothing of fights with the knuckles, but it tolerated and even had a certain tenderness for gloves. So a glove was imagined which had all the deadly stopping power of the naked fist, and at the same time preserved that weapon from going soft with the wear and tear of its own blows. The glove invented for the occasion was so light that it was little more than a second skin, yet it served to give the most deadly contests the excuse of the ' sparring bout,' as distinguished from the fight, and to lead innocent judges and juries into the belief that the glove was the old-fashioned one made on the model of the domestic pillow.

" Under this subterfuge prize-fighting has become the monstrous thing that it now is. It is no longer hunted from pillar to post ; it performs in marble halls or their equivalents, and under the approving eye of the police. It is even more brutal in many respects, for it is now a veritable science of the most deadly and the most disabling blows, with a diminution of the intervals between the rounds, which gives no time for recovery. There is a kidney punch which may be described in its horrible effects as Bright's Disease while you wait. There is a heart punch which is almost sudden death when it gets fairly home. There is a liver punch of the same austerely scientific adaptation of means to an end. If there is no longer the language of the old ring side, there is something worse in all the paraphernalia of social propriety—the evening dress and the cold-blooded satisfaction of a class who need these stimulants to give a pulse to their torpid lives.

" It is really worse now than ever it was, just because it is better in the externals that do not count, and it is still as ever it was in essentials—an epitome of all the blackguardism of sport under new forms that make it the perfection of hypocrisy from first to last. If a modern fight could be seen at close quarters in the colours of nature, as they now do the thing at the establishment of the kinemacolor, I venture to say the ignoble art—for such it is and ever has been—would never recover the blow."

This bit of public service led Meyer into other protests more or less successful, against certain theatrical performances and Sunday games. He came to see in after years that there was very little to be gained unless the Church of Christ witnessed as a whole against such things, stirring the conscience of the community and making action by authorities imperative. But to the end he rejoiced in having stopped a prize fight.

CHAPTER TWELVE

WITH STUDENTS

AFTER Mr. Meyer began to speak at the Keswick Convention he had constant invitations to visit student centres, and found that the messages he was able to give were specially applicable to the student mind and life. He dealt not so much with doctrine as with practical life, and the record is that nobody else was so much blessed in dealing with the men at that time as he was. This was especially true at Cambridge.

The Northfield Convention suggested to him the desirability of some form of training for men different from that given in the ordinary theological colleges, and his experience at University centres gave emphasis to the need. Moody's Bible Training Institute at Chicago, and the Bible Training Institute at Glasgow, which Mr. Moody established, now presided over with so much distinction by Dr. McIntyre, were the type of training required. And as his influence increased he was being constantly asked to advise eager young souls, who felt the Call of God, and did not quite know how to fit themselves for the task.

So, when he first came to Christ Church he started in a very modest way an Institution of his own, known as the South London Missionary Training College, and for three years presided over it with considerable success. The house chosen for the purpose was situated in St. Agnes Place, Kennington Park, a quiet, secluded spot within easy reach of Christ Church : and like a wise man he called in a band of competent helpers, of whom the Rev. James Douglas was the most prominent, to take the oversight of the work. He himself was in constant touch with it, visiting at least twice a week, arriving often as early as eight o'clock on

Monday morning, as if he had had no Sunday work. Sometimes when he was unable to come, the monitor of the college waited on him at Christ Church with the report of the week's work.

A thorough knowledge of the Bible was the chief aim, but New Testament Greek was taught, and English literature, of course. The college continued in being for three years—1893 to 1896, with some fourteen students at a time who received their board and training without charge, often, no doubt, at the expense of their President. During the history of the college some forty men passed through the classes, staying for a longer or shorter time. A large proportion of these went forth as missionaries, and some have done notable work ; amongst them the Rev. Charles Fairclough, now the Principal of the Training College for Evangelists at Hungchow, Chekiang, in connection with the China Inland Mission, where there is accommodation for thirty students ; the Rev. Herbert Halliwell, who after some years successful service in India for Sunday Schools, came home to be the General Secretary of the Christian Endeavour Federation of Great Britain and Ireland ; the Rev. Alec Banks, who for many years has exerted a splendid influence amongst Indian boys in Siwan, in connection with the Regions Beyond Missionary Union. Every year, until the end of his life, Dr. Meyer wrote as far as possible to his former students.

But he soon found from experience that his effort was neither intensive nor extensive enough, and it seemed wiser to merge it in the Regions Beyond Missionary College, of which he then became Vice-President, having for years been a constant visitor to Harley House, Bow, and a fast friend of Dr. Grattan Guinness, its founder, and of his son, Dr. Harry Grattan Guinness, then its President. Of Mr. and Mrs. Guinness, senior, it is unnecessary to speak ; they were both unique, their researches in prophecy and their enterprise in missions being part of the common inheritance of the Church. Of their son, the estimate of his sister, who became the wife of Hudson Taylor's son, Howard, is enough —" Harry is a splendour ! "

In Meyer's Leicester days Harry Guinness was a frequent visitor, as indeed all the Guinness family were at intervals. Emulating my colleague in evangelistic work, Harry learnt to lead the singing with the cornet : on one occasion when a man was hanged in Leicester gaol, and a great crowd of people assembled, Meyer and he held a service at the gaol gates ! At an earlier time I may perhaps be permitted to say that he came to be best man at my wedding.

When he went to Tasmania in 1892, Mr. Meyer, in his absence, guided the college, and took a very practical share in its affairs in the years following, especially when Dr. Harry was visiting the Congo ; and in 1901, when both Dr. and Mrs. Guinness were absent, he came into residence at Harley House, spending each mid-week there, taking prayers every morning and presiding at the Friday afternoon prayer meeting, as well as being at hand to advise the students and supervise the college. Mrs. Heywood Smith, who was in charge of the Guinness family during the absence of their parents, recalls with glee the Christmas party he gave to the children.

Some years later, through the influence of Mr. Geoffrey Thomas, the "All Nations Bible College" was opened at Beulah Hill, Upper Norwood. Dr. Meyer, being then without pastoral charge, was invited to be its first Principal, and came into residence there. From Australia he called to his aid, as Vice-Principal, Mr. James T. Arthur, who had had many years' experience in the Bible Training Institute at Glasgow, and a very happy fellowship subsisted between the two men, as may be judged by extracts from some letters written to Mr. and Mrs. Arthur appended to this chapter. But two serious trials awaited him ; for three months he lay very seriously ill in the college, as the result of the strenuous Australian tour undertaken previously, and at the end of the year difference of opinion as to its management compelled both Mr. Arthur and himself to resign. The present Principal, the Rev H. S Curr, who was called from Macmaster University, is carrying on the work with much encouragement

To Mr. and Mrs. Arthur, on August 15th, 1924, he wrote :

" It was delightful to get your letter, and I feel that time and distance make no difference to the true affection which must ever subsist between us. I love to think of you among the owls, moths, squirrels and butterflies. A holiday like that is a real holiday almost a holy-day. One does feel that God is near one in those natural scenes. It has been one of the mistakes of my life that I have not had such entire unbendings of the bow. That Jubilee year, and the seventh-year-rest, were great institutions for the Hebrews. I wonder how they spent them. Did they fish ? . . . . We did not spend that year at Beulah Hill without commensurate results."

The next day he wrote to Mrs. Arthur acknowledging a letter :

" It was a gracious and mysterious Providence tnat brought us together, and incidentally to the good work that we were able to do for the Master, this additional joy was added of knitting our hearts in friendship . . . Among the fish what rejoicing there will be when your husband's dexterous hand and rod no longer beguile their fathers, mothers, and friends . . . How much there is to learn before we really become conformed to the Image of the Son. One would despair, except it were for the fact that we are under the moulding hands of a Father, whose patience is infinite."

On September 30th he writes :

" It is a deep pleasure to know that you and your dear wife are where you are loved and understood. The Beulah Hill experience one can never forget . . . It gave me your comradeship, and Dr. Smallwood and the dear lady, and the beautiful room in which to be ill . . . It is rather beautiful to be reaping on little patches, or single leaves, the seed sown years ago. God is so good in this, but I am deeply in debt which only the Blood of Christ could discharge. I miss those talks we used to have, and know of no one with whom I can have such happy sympathy. Everywhere the hearts of men are failing them for fear, but it is a beautiful outlook that we shall be ere long finding ' some humble home amid the many mansions, some sheltering shade where sin and sorrow cease.' "

A letter undated follows :

" It was really delightful to have your letter with its tidings about yourselves, and the lads whom we have watched over, loved and sent forth. It was a very beautiful Providence that brought us together, and though we are scattered in our outward seeming, the inner fellowship will always endure."

On August 26th, 1925, this :

" I hope you are on holiday, and that *he* is learning how to fish for souls by the experience gained on the banks of a river or stream. You wrote me such a sweet letter when I was starting for Canada. I have it before me, and this is an answer to that and needs no further reply. The Canadian visit will yield blessed results, I think. Indeed, I have heard already of some, and the subsequent Conventions at Llandrindod, Morges, and Malvern have all yielded fruit. At Morges it was good to meet the young Frenchman whom we sent to help Pastor Blocher. Naturally we talked about Beulah Hill."

The letter dated November 30th, 1925, is brief :

" It was very welcome to get news of the boys through your letter. They were exceptionally fine material, and their intimate relations were as formative as the lectures. It was a beautiful time to which I often look back. I am keeping fairly well ! I am so inspired just now with the thought—' Your Father, who is in secret.' "

On December 2nd, 1927, after thanks and greetings, he wrote :

" A mosquito bite, on the top of an over-tired heart, sent me into a nursing home for three weeks. I am now much better but am resting until the New Year. Alas ! that the Tent is getting rather old and dilapidated. Would that I had all my years given back, *with the experience* of these later years. The Church badly needs to understand her wonderful heritage. What lovely talks we had, and *shall have*."

And then a wish, twice repeated, and expressed to other kindred spirits :

" You dear souls ! I do love you, and we must have a thousand years in Heaven. Let us meet at the middle gate on the Eastern aspect of the city, and then a picnic amid the Fountain of Waters."

CHAPTER THIRTEEN

WITH YOUTH

WHEN it is remembered that at Leicester Mr. Meyer had no less than 2,500 Sunday scholars under his care, and at Christ Church the oversight of 4,000 in eight Sunday Schools, one of them established by Rowland Hill when he first came to Surrey Chapel in 1785, it is not surprising that his interest in young people was lifelong.

Early in his ministry in London he devoted Saturday afternoons for eight months each year to a meeting in the Aldersgate Street Young Men's Christian Association Hall, at which, to a considerable and deeply interested company of young men, he expounded the International Sunday School lesson for the following day. The gatherings were most informal, and they are gratefully remembered by many to-day, not only for the help they gave for the immediate need of the class, but for the direction they indicated for the whole Christian outlook.

One of the members of this class was Dr. F. W. Boreham, of Melbourne, Australia, who, in all parts of the world, has testified to the lasting impressions made on those Saturday afternoons. " I have often wondered," says Dr. Boreham, " how any man would get on nowadays who attempted to run a Bible Class for Young Men on Saturday afternoons ! But Dr. Meyer did it, and every Saturday some hundreds of young fellows flocked to him at Aldersgate Street. I seem to see him now as he sat on his high stool at his table below us—for the seats sloped up from him—pouring out to us the treasures of his deep experience. Every now and again he would become excited by his theme, and with an ' Oh, my brothers, I want to tell you . . . ' he would leave the stool and with eyes sparkling and hands gesticulating, would pace up and down the floor before us. I really think that we lived for those Saturday afternoons. We counted

the hours till they came ; and, as each passed, its influence
abode upon us like a perfume. I am so glad that when
Dr. Meyer was in Australia I had the opportunity of telling
him of this.

" I often think of his extraordinary sympathy with
young strugglers. Personally, I always had a penchant for
scribbling ; and, whilst I was yet in my teens, so far forgot
myself as to write a small book ! With fear and trembling
I took the manuscript to a firm of publishers in Paternoster
Row. ' Well,' they said, probably thinking that they were
playing for safety by making an impossible condition,
' we will publish it if Dr. F. B. Meyer will write the
Introduction to it ! ' Here was a poser ! Dr. Meyer was one
of the best known men in London, whilst I was utterly
unknown—to him and to everybody else ! True, I was in
the habit of attending his Saturday afternoon Bible Class ;
but how should he know that ? I was only one of hundreds
who came and went without making themselves known to
him. However, nothing venture, nothing win ! I posted
the manuscript that night to Dr. Meyer with a report of
the publisher's stipulation. By return of post he sent me
an *Introduction* written with his own hand ! I was overwhelmed ; the publisher was astounded ; and the book
was published, although, happily for everybody concerned,
it has now been for many years out of print ! "

The following Resolution tells its own story :—" The
Committee of the City of London Young Men's Christian
Association, in recording the Home Call of its beloved
Vice-President, Dr. F. B. Meyer, desire to express their
sense of the loss which has befallen this Association in
common with the Work of God in all lands.

" Dr. Meyer's radiant personality, spiritual fervour,
inspiring devotion and intense sympathy, with his passionate
love for the souls of men, especially endeared him to young
manhood. From those early days of business life within
the gates of London City until his departure for that City
whose Builder and Maker is God, this Centre enjoyed his
warm affection and received his unstinted service.

" His Saturday afternoon Bible Exposition of the International Sunday School Lessons attracted hundreds of young men weekly for upwards of fourteen years, passing them on to their respective Churches as teachers freighted with the rich things of God to the eternal blessing of multitudes of children under their care. Although started with the object of providing efficient Sunday School teachers, this gathering proved fruitful also in large numbers of young men being ' born from above,' the service thus demonstrating the determined purpose of the Y.M.C.A. to co-operate and not to compete with the Churches of God."

With this experience nothing was more natural than that Mr. Meyer should be elected by the National Sunday School Union in 1902 as its first ministerial President. During his year of office Rev. Carey Bonner says that he rendered pre-eminent service by a generous expenditure of time and thought, paying numerous visits to the various parts of the kingdom giving addresses that were a never-failing source of inspiration. At the end of his year of office he was appointed as one of the Vice-Presidents, and on many occasions he helped the Union both by speech and pen.

At the World's Fifth Sunday School Convention, held at Rome in May, 1907, Mr. Meyer was elected as President of the World's Sunday School Association, and took a considerable share in the proceedings of the gathering. In a sermon on " The Oneness of Believers," he said, " I find in my own ministry that supposing I pray for my own little flock, God bless me, God fill my pews, God send me a revival, I miss the blessing, but as I pray for my big brother, Mr. Spurgeon, on the right-hand side of my church, God bless him ; or my other big brother Campbell Morgan, on the other side of my church, God bless him, I am sure to get a blessing without praying for it, for the overflow of their cups fills my little bucket."

A memorable service was held in the Coliseum in Rome on May 23rd. " There, with the old brown walls about us, and the arena close beside us, this world-gathering of Christians, without molestation, sang its hymns and prayed under the open sky where once our predecessors of high faith and unfaltering courage were prey for lions or wilder beasts of men." Mr. Meyer's share was the reading of an impressive poem of twenty eight-line stanzas, " The Architect of the Amphitheatre," composed for the occasion by Rev. Walter J. Mathams. " This poem made a deep impression on the delegates, not because of its historical accuracy, but on account of its author's vivid rendering of his thought, and the exceptional circumstances of its utterance."

The following year found Dr. Meyer in the Chair at the great gathering at Washington and right worthily he rose to the occasion. Perhaps the most notable incident of the Conference was the visit of President Taft, who came on the platform with a little lady who took a seat on one of the back rows. Dr. Meyer went to her side and insisted that she should come to the front, and amid tremendous applause from the thousands present led her to her husband's side, who thereupon introduced her to the delegates as the real President of the United States.

The Convention Sermon on " The Possibilities of Child Life," from the text Psalms viii. 2, struck a high note. " The universe is big," said Dr. Meyer, " but the child is Great." A great passage in the discourse was the contrast between the two types of religion. " The first is that of the understanding, of tradition, of the unchanging shibboleth, of outward ceremonial : very clever, very exacting, very precise : every i dotted, every t crossed. It is the religion of the schools, the creeds, the heritage of church councils, the result of the tangled arenas of theological dispute. Will these formularies still the enemy and avenger ? Never I The body may be carefully posed, equipped in mail, and yet be dead, the hand nerveless, the eye lustreless.

" The second is the religion of the heart—reflecting such glimpses of eternal Truth and Beauty, which are possible to men. The Love that is attracted by nobility and purity : the Thought that is so deep because so artless : the Faith that finds resistless reason in the beauty and goodness of things : the Humility that takes the lowest place : the

Snow-white Innocence that becomes purity of flame : the Forgiveness that takes no account of evil. The one is the religion of the man, the other of the child." And there were not wanting some who, that day, thought that he himself was the Child.

By resolution of the House of Representatives of the United States then in session the House adjourned on the twentieth of May at four o'clock as the parade of members and delegates was to pass before the East front of the Capitol at five, "as a mark of respect to the delegates assembled, as well as to the Cause which they represent, and for the further purpose of permitting members of the House who may desire to do so, to participate in the said parade." Imagine the House of Commons doing that in honour of Sunday Schools !

Early in the Conference there was a good deal of disturbance by the stupid habit some of the delegates had formed, of sampling the speaker and then passing out in the midst of his address. Dr. Meyer, a master of assemblies, determined to stop the practice, so at the next session he announced that those who wished to leave must do so before the speaker began. Either misunderstanding or rebelling, a number of persons, chiefly women, rose to go after the speaker had been five minutes on his feet, but they misjudged their man. Dr. Meyer called a pause, commanded the door stewards to keep the doors shut, and told those who were passing down the aisles that they must return to their seats— and in sheer surprise they obeyed. Every one, even the delinquents, admired his gentle firmness, and there was no further interruption of that sort.

The final word of the Convention which he uttered was a model of dignity and deep feeling :—

" Depart ye, go ye out from hence : be ye clean that bear the vessels of the Lord. For you shall not go out in haste, nor go by flight : for the Lord shall go before you : and the Holy One of Israel shall be your rereward. Arise, let us go hence."

And then a great Benediction invoking the peace of

God on " ourselves, our homes, our schools, our churches, our countries, and the One Church of God throughout the world."

Prior to the Washington Congress Dr. Meyer, accompanied by Mr. Marion Lawrance and Mr. E. O. Excell, had an extended tour of some two months through the United States to advocate Sunday School work, travelling some eight thousand miles and leaving a trail of blessing behind them. " From New York to Texas," he said, " the success of the tour has been most marked. Our object was not only to deepen the interest in Sunday School work, but to raise a fund for the extension of Sunday School movements throughout the world. For this purpose we have secured about £20,000."

At Zurich in July, 1913, having retired from his Presidency, Dr. Meyer gave no less than eight inspirational addresses, and those who were privileged to be present declare that they were the most spiritually powerful that they have ever heard. At the Keswick Convention which immediately followed some notable testimonies were given of the blessing received, one well-known Christian leader declaring that it had been the means of his conversion.

Dr. Meyer himself, preaching at Christ Church the following Sunday, confessed that he had embarked for the Continent afflicted with gloom, induced by the emphasis which was then being laid on " the arrested progress " of the Church, and the dislocation of the ancient habits of religion, but Zurich had not only dispersed his depression but had given him a new hope and a new vision. Zurich itself was the prolific home of Protestantism, Puritanism and Pietism, and it had now given them a new thought— the world was to be won through the child.

During his later ministry, Dr. Meyer for some time resumed his exposition of the International lessons on Saturdays, at the Sunday School Union Hall in Old Bailey, and, still later, in a series of Thursday evening services at Christ Church, gathered a great company of teachers for the same purpose.

At the Baptist Assembly at Glasgow Mr. Meyer, on October 6th, 1910, gave an encyclopædic address on " Improved Sunday School Methods and Reform," which does not lend itself to analysis because it is all so practically useful. But a few quotations may be given.

" It is narrated that Dr. Horace Bushnell on one occasion asked his friend, Henry Clay Trumbull if he were not devoting too much time and strength to his Sunday School. That ardent Sunday School enthusiast vigorously repudiated the suggestion, and years after Dr. Bushnell, referring to the conversation, said, ' Trumbull, you knew better than I did, where the Lord wanted you. I honestly thought the pulpit was a bigger place for you, and tried to get you into it : but now I've come to see that the work you are doing is the greatest work in the world.' And after a moment's pause, he added, ' Sometimes I think that it is the only work there is in the world.' "

" We have not understood child-nature. The prevailing notion seems to be that the only difference between the child and the adult is one of degree, rather than of kind. *We say* that a child is plastic clay, only waiting to be moulded. *But it isn't so.* There is a spirit behind the clay. *We say* that he is a block of marble to be hewn according to the sculptor's will. *But it isn't so.* There is soul in those marble depths. *We say* that the boy is a little man. *But it isn't so.* Professor Adams says, ' The boy is no more a little man than the grub is a little butterfly or the tadpole a little frog.' "

It is worthy of note that during the last year of his life he doubled his subscription to the W.S.S.A. and sent it with an expression of his deep interest in its missionary work.

His association with the Society of Christian Endeavour was long and honourable. He was elected as President of the National Union in Belfast in 1900 and in company with his intimate friend, the Rev. James Mursell, he encouraged the various branches of the Endeavour Society, which was then in the hey-day of its success, in all parts of the country.

Let Mr. Mursell himself tell the story. In glowing words
he writes :—

" The Whitsuntide of 1888 is for ever memorable to me
because it was the first time I saw and heard him, and was
sent home with the cry in my heart, ' I will never rest till
I learn the secret that man has learnt ' ; and I could name
day, hour and place at which some words of his, simple,
yet tremendous in their import, brought into my life an
experience of blessing and power that still overflows it.

" It is no exaggeration to say that multitudes could bear
the same witness concerning him. He was a very human
being, and it was by no means difficult for critics to find
flaws in him, but this may be said of him with soberness and
truth, that few public men of his day and generation lived
nearer to God, and did so much real good, and gave so
much real help to people who wanted honestly and practically
to live Christ-like lives.

" It has been my happy lot to share the intimacies of
his home—I saw him last less than three months ago in
it—to travel far by land and sea with him, to stand on
public platforms at his side ; and to be with him was
always benediction. He sent me away with a fire in my
heart and a light in my sky ; better, or at least wanting
to be so, because I had been with him. This again is a
testimony that thousands could give ; and what finer
tribute could be paid to any man than to say that he helped
them Godward ?

" It was this and the intensely practical mysticism of
his addresses that drew young lives round him. He was a
man of speculative mind, intensely interested in ideas ;
but that was a side he showed to very few, and rarely even
to them. His supreme interests were God and man, Jesus
Christ and common or garden people. His appeal to
Christian Endeavourers and his influence over them had
its secret here. He was a triumphant Endeavourer whose
life was hidden with Christ in God and who was obviously
to men and women, and especially to the young, out and out
for Him.

" I think I am right in saying that he was the first man to come to the British presidency of the movement who was not a member of the National Council. And what a President he made ! He gave two days, one might almost say two days and two nights, a week to visiting Endeavour centres. He always had two companions, and his most frequent associates were Miss Weatherley, as she then was, or Miss Jennie Street, and myself.

" The programme usually included a lunch with ministers, a service at which he preached, a conference at which he presided, his colleagues spoke, and he gathered up the threads ; a tea-table conference conducted by him with immense gusto and delightful abandon, and then a public meeting at which, after addresses to young men and to young women by the others, he spoke to both and gave a talk on everyday living that for glancing humour, homely wisdom, experimental reality and searching, almost agonising power, I have never heard surpassed. If all now living who received definite impulses towards nobler life through those addresses could meet, they would, I am convinced, overcrowd the biggest hall in London. He always gave the same address and insisted that we should do the same.

" Often we got back to London in the small hours, and after a cup of coffee at a stall just outside King's Cross he would carry me off to his own home, that mine should not be disturbed. On our journeys he would read or dictate an article, and wearying in the midst of it would say, ' I think I'll sleep,' to drop off in a moment, and in ten minutes wake refreshed and dictate the rest of the article as if he had never paused."

Of his own experiences he wrote in after years to Mr. Mursell :

" Chicago, 15th April, 1910.
" MY VERY DEAR FRIEND.

" Without laying down rules for others, I realise that the spiritual is my special realm, and that I must use all my time in that direction during the afternoon of my ministry. A man must conserve himself for his best work last, and for this he must do what he can do best.

" So it is good for this break to have come in my life, which enables me to begin over again. Of course, it is through political action that we register the moral advance of our nation, and we cannot ignore its importance, but, as for me, I think, if I must choose, it will be for the spiritual.

" Yours ever affectionately,

" F. B. MEYER."

" R.M.S. *Campania, June 2nd*, 1910.

" MY DEAR, DEAR FRIEND,

" Your two letters are very fragrant. Thanks. Thanks. Here I am not far from New York. I have so enjoyed this voyage having a cabin to myself. I want to understand better what it is to have God's nature rising up and filling me from unknown depths, if not consciously to my feelings, yet very real to my Faith. Even if that infilling does not register itself in intellectual processes or emotion I am sure that it leaves, and is, a very substantial residuum that manifests itself ultimately in deed.

" I have so enjoyed your letter breathing of leisure and peace. I feel so deeply the need of these, and am resolved when I have got through my present engagements to see whether I cannot live more as the Lord lived, taking the Father's will from hour to hour. This cut and dried system cannot be the best for us. I am well, thank God, and don't feel to be in my sixty-fifth year.

" Yours ever affectionately,

" F. B. MEYER."

In 1911 he was President of the London Federation of Christian Endeavour and carried through a campaign extending from September to April, 1912, afternoon and evening meetings being held generally on the Saturday of each week, in a score of districts, with a great array of speakers. The whole culminated in the Annual Convention on Good Friday in Spurgeon's Tabernacle. Mr. Meyer presided all through and his unvarying subject was " Personal Consecration."

A Young People's Society of Christian Endeavour at Los Angeles has issued on a card a dedication for the day abridged from " Saved and Kept," by Dr. Meyer, in order that profounder prayer may lead to nobler lives.—

As I Stand on the Doorway of this New Day I come to Thee, most blessed Lord, to renew my vows. My soul lies low in penitence before Thee, as I recall all Thy patience and lovingkindness. I solemnly renounce and put away the evil things which have usurped an unholy supremacy with me—the companionships, books and amusements that have cast a shadow on my hours of fellowship ; the sin that so easily besets me ; the soft yielding to sloth ; the desire to please men rather than Thee, and to succeed in this world rather than to be Thy humble servant. In myself, I cannot keep these resolutions ; my will is like a bruised reed. O keep Thou me from unfaithfulness !

In My Inner Life I desire to be kept absolutely pure and lovely. O Holy and Spotless One, be in me the crystal fountain of purity ! O Lamb of God, be in me the source of absolute meekness and humility ! O Lover of men, be in me a fire of unwaning and all-subduing tenderness ! Make me sensitive to any uncharity.

In My Home Life may I be a blessing ; a tender comfort when days are full of pain ; always thinking of others before myself, and never imposing upon them my private sorrows or moods.

In My Daily Calling make me diligent in business, fervent in spirit, serving the Lord. May I work not for the wages I may receive, or for advancement, but so as to please Jesus, my Master. May I do all to the glory of God ; not with eye-service as pleasing men ; but in singleness of heart fearing the Lord. In my use of money, I would not be anxious about the future or hoard for myself. I want to use all things as Thy steward.

In My Use of Time, Health, and the Opportunities of Life I desire to act with reverent care ; conserving my body as the pure temple of the Holy Ghost ; so partaking of recreation that I may better serve Thy purpose in my creation and redemption. Teach me what my talents are, and help me to make the two four and the five ten. Through Jesus Christ, our Lord. Amen.

His interest in children is emphasised in a descriptive paragraph from *John O' London's Weekly*, July 12th, 1924 : " His body is tall and spare, alert and straight. The face is pale and clean shaven, the beautifully moulded features combining to a wonderful degree a look of dignity, peace and holiness. Solemnity (not gloom) is the prevailing expression, but frequently the face lights up with the most winning of smiles. There is something wonderfully sympathetic and fascinating in the character and personality of Dr. Meyer. He loves the beauty of the world, he loves animals, and above all he loves little children. These things he never succeeds in concealing from us, however hard he may try, and they peep out from every sermon or address that he delivers."

To the Rev. E. Palgrave Davy Dr. Meyer wrote :

" DEAR DAVY, *July 16th*, 1918.

" I have got terribly behind with my correspondence, but there are no arrears in my affectionate remembrance of you. Your letter, with its interesting and ingenious diagrams, shows how absolutely you are fitted for this work among children, boys and girls. God has led you by His own right hand to the place He had prepared, and I am so glad to have had a wee share in it. As you ladle the water out to the children, may He work the miracle of Cana on each act, and as one of the servants, you will know. The servants, who draw the water, always have an insight, denied to others. See the bracket in John ii.

" Yours ever affectionately,

" F. B. MEYER."

But it was with the children themselves that he was at his best. At Christ Church he always had a Christmas party for " The Brotherhood " children, and the next day a gala supper for the children of the congregation, including the children of missionaries and others. In his later years he often explained to the young folk that life was a circle and he had gone round it so far that he was back again nearly to the place where he started, so he and they were very close together, and that he understood them much better than middle-aged people could, which indeed was the case. He kept the child heart all through.

CHAPTER FOURTEEN

WITH MISSIONARIES

WITH much approval Dr. Meyer often quoted the dictum of Phillips Brooks when he was asked what he would do to revive a decadent Church. He replied instantly, " I would preach a missionary sermon and take up a collection."

" It is often a wonder to me," Mr. Meyer wrote in the *Medical Missionary* for January, 1910, " that so few, comparatively, of our Christian youth volunteer as missionaries. Of course it may be that they are.withheld by the same considerations as withheld me in my own young life. Those were the days of William Knibb, Robert Moffatt and David Livingstone and others whose names are household words. Like stars they were shining in the dark sky of heathenism. The inspiration of their words was in our home, and to me they seemed the very greatest of men. So profound was my veneration for them that it never entered my head that *I* should become a missionary. That I might become a Christian minister was within the limits of possibility, but to be a missionary—*never*.

" That, of course, was a misconception on my part. There is no reason why those who desire to give up their lives wholly to the service of God should not become missionaries to the heathen, equally as they may become ministers and Christian workers at home. The characters and ideals of the missionaries I have met are, speaking generally, extremely noble and beautiful, and their self-sacrifice exemplary : but there is no such extraordinary difference as would warrant the nervous diffidence I felt."

His world-wide work was in itself missionary; and during his ministry, while interested in all efforts to win the nations, he gave practical help, at different times, to three Missionary Societies. For the London Missionary Society he preached the Annual Missionary Sermon, which was afterwards expanded into a charming little book, " The Wideness of God's Mercy " : and, later, he preached at Leicester the Baptist Missionary Sermon on " The Curse of Meroz."

The B.M.S. was his first love, and though he was never a member of its committee, his presence at one of its earliest Summer Schools, which was held at Folkestone in July, 1910, put him in touch with the inner circle of its influence. He took five services at that school and " spoke with all his characteristic qualities. His help was very great. He seems to have gained," says the *British Weekly*, " in energy and alertness. He was full of quaint humour and spirituality. He bids fair to become the Father Tauler of the Baptist Churches. It was delightful to see the Bishop of Regent's Park on tramp through the Warren with the young men and women, the most playful of them all." Not content with this bit of missionary service, we find him at the L.M.S. Summer School at Studley Castle, Warwickshire, the following month.

At his various churches, save Christ Church which mainly supported the L.M.S., he urged the claims of the B.M.S., their own Society as Baptists, though he always had the deepest sympathy with the China Inland Mission, as he had the intimate friendship of Hudson Taylor. From the Leicester Church several recruits went forth at different times in association with the North Africa Mission. And when he was Honorary Secretary of the Free Church Council it was his custom to invite missionaries of all Free Church Societies and the Society of Friends to a yearly Conference.

But his most definite effort for the Enterprise of Christ in the world was made in association with the " Regions Beyond Missionary Union." This was not surprising when it is remembered that he had such early and close association with Dr. Grattan Guinness and with Harley House.

It was, perhaps, during his visit to his friend, Mr. Hugh Brown, in July, 1920, at Skelmorlie, that his final decision was made. His host says, " He arrived on the Saturday evening. What a beautiful night it was, with the sun setting over the Arran hills ! We could not get him away from the window where he knelt gazing at the sunset. I well remember how a remark by some one brought forth a kindly rebuke that they were not to take his gaze away from the sunset.

" On the Sunday morning he preached in one of the churches, and in the afternoon he went up to Kelly, and visited the hut built by Susi and Chummah, the two African followers of Livingstone who conveyed his body home. They were invited by the late Mr. Young of Kelly, who was a friend of Livingstone, to come and stay with him, and when there he got them to erect a facsimile hut to the one in which Livingstone died. Dr. Meyer returned home at tea-time greatly impressed with what he had seen."

" Speaking of this two or three years later at St. George's Cross Tabernacle, Glasgow." says the Memorial Number of the *Regions Beyond*, " Dr. Meyer said that he requested all the others to leave him alone in the hut, and there, kneeling by the bedside, he re-dedicated his life to the Lord for the furtherance of the Gospel in heathen lands."

Soon after this he became Acting Director and General Secretary of the R.B.M.U., and practically for the remainder of his life devoted much time to promote the work in Congo and in India, for which the Society is responsible. Nothing indeed would have pleased him more than to visit the Congo region, and to die there, as a new claim on Africa for Christ.

His service during these later years on behalf of the Society was intimate and detailed. He would spend four hours several days of the week in the office directing affairs : he presided, with full knowledge, at the meetings of the Committee : spoke on its behalf in this country and abroad ;

and by that means brought in many gifts for its funds.
Nothing pleased him more than to visit the beautiful Home
which the R.B.M.U. maintains for missionaries' Children,
except perhaps to share in the Easter Conferences it convened at Slavanka, near Bournemouth. It was probably a
half-conscious desire to be present at the latest of these
conferences which in his last illness made him eager to get
down to Bournemouth, for he had no idea then that the
illness was his last.

To the Chairman of the Board of Directors he sent the
following letter on March 24th, 1929, signing it with his own
hand :

" DEAR MR. ECCLES,

" The doctors say that my life is nearing its close and may at
any time end. I desire, therefore, to send my parting message
to yourself, our Council, and our noble band of missionaries.
Almost from the first day of its inception I have been identified
with the R.B.M.U., and I am thankful that under your wise
guidance, combined with the splendid service of Rev. H. S.
Gamman, it has come to a pitch of efficiency which we never
dreamt of in the earlier days.

" I may be meeting very soon hundreds of men and women
who are the result of our joint efforts.

" In taking leave of yourself and our Council, I want to
express my deep gratitude for the kind manner in which they
have always met me.

" Again wishing you increasing success and God's richest
blessing on your efforts,

" Yours very sincerely,

" F. B. MEYER."

The following tribute from the Rev. J. Ireland Hasler,
missionary in India since 1892, may fitly close this chapter :
" My first acquaintance with Dr. Meyer was made years
ago through those penny booklets which he wrote dealing
with some of the essential conditions for a strong religious
life, and when in 1891 I came to live in London, I joined
his church.

" From the very outset he put me into Christian service. In those days he used to have a Men's Meeting on Sunday afternoons at Regent's Park Chapel, and this was followed by a cheap tea for the benefit of those who lived at a distance or in the loneliness of lodgings. One afternoon I had attended the meeting and stayed on for the tea. He noticed the stranger and called me to him, and after ascertaining who I was, asked me if I had ever visited a lodging-house. If not, I should be able to have the opportunity of doing so that evening. I said that I had come to hear him preach. He then enquired if I had attended morning service anywhere and on hearing my reply remarked, ' You've been fed yourself—now go and feed others.' I was then introduced to the leader of the Mission Band which he had inaugurated for the purpose of spending the Sunday evening in services in ' doss-houses,' thieves' kitchens, the open air and Drummond Street Mission Hall. He did not believe in Christians attending his services twice on the Sunday if it was possible for them to be of use to others. From that Mission Band at least seven afterwards went to the foreign field.

" It was when listening to a sermon that he was preaching at Regent's Park Church in the Centenary Year of the Baptist Missionary Society that I received the call to go abroad. He had spoken of the need there was in lands across the sea and then said, ' I do not ask if you have felt a special call to go abroad—the need is the call. Is there anything in your circumstances which hinders you from going ? ' As he said that I saw my life as in a flash of light and felt that I, at any rate, was free to go.

" More than thirty-five years have elapsed since I first went to India. Most furloughs I have met him, at least once, during the time that I happened to be in England. A few years ago I was surprised and gratified to receive a letter from him. He had heard somehow of work that I was doing and thought that some of his books might be of help to some of the Indians with whom I was coming into contact—Indians of the type that are recorded in ' The

Christ of the Indian Road.' And so he sent me a parcel for free distribution.

" He had heard of the probability of my retirement and deprecated it. After my return to England recently I wrote to tell him that I was going back after all. He wrote in reply, ' I seem to want to see you,' and invited my wife and myself to lunch with him in his home. Thirteen years had elapsed since I had previously seen him, and he had aged greatly. He appeared to have grown smaller. The change, however, was only in the outward. The inner personality was still as genial and as impressive as ever. But he had a heavy cold on him—it was the beginning of his fatal illness—and he ought then to have been in bed.

" He had promised, however, to write an article for the *Daily Mail*. He was puzzled as to why the results of Mission work in India were not more on a par with those in Africa. I reminded him that the Kingdom of God was not only likened to a net cast into the sea but also to leaven hid in meal. You could employ numerical calculations in the one case but not in the other. The parable of the leaven appeared especially to illustrate the method of the Divine operation in India. Ere we left he spoke of the religious life in England. He felt that there was a deepening of the religious spirit outside the pale of the Church—indeed, he appeared to feel more hopeful about the people outside the Church than those within, if I have not mistaken his meaning. I told him that I thought he had answered his own question about India. In the national life and activities of India there were increasing evidences of the influence of the Spirit of Christ.

" I write these experiences not because I think they are unique but because I think they are typical. The number of young men and women who, through contact with his life, were led into different forms of Christian service at home or abroad, must be beyond reckoning. In their work his work will be continued to some extent.

" But as there was only one C. H. Spurgeon, there has been only one F. B. Meyer. Time was when I felt if I could hear him preach only once on a Sunday it would keep me living aright during the week. And then there came his first visit to America, during which strangers would occupy his pulpit. The prospect filled me with dismay. ' Men and women,' he said, in a sermon before sailing, ' you can do without me : you cannot do without *God.*' That is the great service he did for the innumerable company of which I am but one—he linked us to God.

CHAPTER FIFTEEN

THE INSURGENCE OF SEX

PROBABLY we are more sane than our fathers in our attitude to the essential difference between men and women, of which their outer form is only the expression : more sane, more open in our speech, and more conscious of its inherent rightness. But to safeguard its rightness we are also aware that there is increasing need of restraint, and consequently more need of enlightenment and of warning. Not every occasion and not every man is fitted for the public discussion of the matter. Dr. Meyer, who desired to touch life at all points, felt the call and found frequent occasion to speak. Only those who know the discipline of sex have the right to speak of its insurgence, and he had earned that right by his own experience.

A well-known doctor in a northern city who writes to me over his own name, but desires to remain anonymous if his letter is quoted, says, " The following incident, narrated briefly, may be of interest to you. It occurred in September, 1900. I requested the favour of an interview with him after a Sunday evening service at Christ Church. He said that he was very tired but would give me a few minutes.

" In explaining my trouble, I mentioned that I had been engaged in work for Christ for several years but had suddenly been plunged into spiritual darkness and great and painful distress after following what I thought to be the guidance obtained by prayer. He advised me not to give up Christian work. ' God has permitted it ' ; and then under strong emotion he jumped from his chair, took a few paces, raised and clasped his hands. His face was transformed, and looking upward he said with intense fervour,

' I have had a cross to bear in my life, and it has made me the man I am.'

" I was awed. I shall never forget it. I thanked him for his advice and withdrew. This self-revelation of the life of such a great man I have considered sacred until now I took his advice, continued in Christian work, increased in activities, and took up my cross with a changed outlook."

*   *   *   *   *

Soon after Exeter Hall in the Strand was acquired, largely through the generosity of Sir George Williams, by the Young Men's Christian Association, Mr. Meyer gave a series of talks to young men on " Personal Purity," which drew large audiences. This effort was afterwards developed by Mr. Henry Varley and Dr. Harry Grattan Guinness, and Mr. Meyer wrote several short arresting booklets on the subject, each with a picture on the outside—one, asking young men to think, had a picture of a young fellow holding his head in his hand ; another, an older man taking a young man's arm ; and so on.

For about ten years, Mr. Clarence Hooper, who was then one of the Exeter Hall Secretaries, reports, Gospel Temperance Meetings were held monthly in many of the wholesale warehouses within the city, and in these Mr. Meyer largely shared. All through the years he continued under various auspices to give addresses to men only in many parts of the country, sometimes in conjunction with other speakers, often in meetings specially convened for himself alone.

This sort of advocacy has its perils unless undertaken in a purely scientific temper or surrounded by a deeply spiritual sentiment. It often suggests the very evils it seeks to combat. The Apostle Paul rang true to human nature as he wrote, " When the commandment came sin revived and I died." Innocence is not holiness, knowledge is essential to right living, but in getting light we may kindle sparks, and even sparks are dangerous where there is tinder or gunpowder. The body may even respond to intense spiritual emotion, the whole nature acting together under unaccustomed excitement.

This being granted and guarded against, Mr. Meyer ventured to take the risk. I am not sure that he always succeeded, though he generally spoke clearly and cleanly enough. But that he often accomplished his purpose is evidenced by an instance, recorded in a Nottingham newspaper, which we may believe is only a sample of others. The anonymous writer says :

" I was at that time a provincial-bred youth in London. On a lonely Sunday afternoon (and Heaven alone knows how lonely a Sunday afternoon can be to a youth, a stranger in the Metropolis) I was impelled to attend a meeting (I cannot remember now even where it was) announced as for men and youths only.

" The Rev. F. B. Meyer was the speaker. I had not seen him before, I have not seen him since.

" I remember him, even then, as a grey-haired, kindly-faced old man, but of so gentle a dignity that instead of the giggle or self-conscious smirk which the topics, discussed by any other man, would have raised in me, every word from his grave lips entered my consciousness and my memory deeper and more enduring than any moral lesson I ever received from teacher, friend, or even parents.

" His method was dramatic. His audience, more than a thousand men and youths, were on their knees with bowed heads and averted eyes for the whole half hour of his address.

" His topics were brutally intimate ; his maxims, warnings and appeals deliberately crude to the point almost of coarseness. I know not what was the effect on the thousand others who knelt with me that Sunday afternoon.

" I realise only that no man I ever met or listened to taught me so much of myself, or provided me with a more powerful and sophisticated barrier against the rampant temptation to vileness, or who exercised so powerful and lasting an influence on my life."

*   *   *   *   *

But Dr. Meyer was not content with warning, he sought to reclaim. Christ Church is close to a district that was long accounted as the moral cesspool of London. It was impossible for a man with his sensibilities to acquiesce in that state of things, and he found others willing to join him in a crusade to claim the neighbourhood. That led to the formation of the Purity, Rescue and Temperance work of the Central South London Free Church Council, which, since its formation, has closed over eleven hundred disreputable houses and rescued many hundreds of women.

Sister Margaret is the soul of the movement, and her deep sympathy, quick humour and strong common sense have gained many a victory when she has been fighting against odds. Her courage and muscular power enable her to face some dangerous situations, she has had more than one black eye given to her, has been struck with heavy sticks and threatened time and again by vicious men whom she has baffled.

Her home is in the midst of the district. On the ground floor she has a large reception room, two rooms thrown into one in fact, with the window flush with the street, but screened by ribbed glass. The walls have some choice pictures on them, Swiss scenes which remind her of her visit to the mountains, portraits of her boys whom she helped in France in the war time, more than one photograph of Dr. Meyer who so largely sustained the work. Best of all is a picture of the Lord Jesus present in a church. The worshippers are up in the light near the chancel, but a penitent woman half-kneeling, half-prone, is in the shadow behind the hindmost seat, and it is there that Christ in shining raiment stands beside her—there with the penitent, who does not count herself worthy to go any further into the sacred building—*there*. And when women visit Sister Margaret in their despair, or when she brings to her home some wanderer from the streets, it is to that picture she takes them, and then there is no need of words. The text beneath the picture is, " Lo, I am with you alway, even to the end of the world," healing words to a woman when everybody else has forsaken her.

It is known far and wide that Sister Margaret has a tea

party every night from one to three o'clock in the morning, and many a wayfarer knocks for admission, or taps on the window, and all of them are welcomed, even when after her tramp through the streets she herself is weary. For she seeks the wanderers, and each year sends scores of them back to their homes.

Sometimes they promise to come to Christ Church on Sunday, and sometimes they come. One young woman after the sermon when Dr. Meyer preached said to Sister as she went out, " Ain't he lovely : he wouldn't condemn you ! " A group of three who were frequently met in Leicester Square came one Sunday morning, and although Dr. Meyer knew nothing about it, he said, " God can make spoiled lives good : let Him make yours good." Two of the girls never returned to their old life, but the third, a well-educated Lancashire girl, went on and drank more heavily than ever. For three months she continued, but she said, " God closed my ears to everything but the preacher's voice saying, ' God can make spoiled lives good.' " She went lower and lower, but still the words pursued her, " God can make spoiled lives good."

After a specially wild night she looked at her money and muttered to herself, " Thou fool ! " But then she remembered that God can make spoiled lives good, and she said, " I'll have a shot at it." She had been the head of a department in a business house : she went to another in the same business, and got a situation as a subordinate assistant. But soon she earned promotion, and day by day she proved that God could keep her in spite of her past.

" One night she went to Leicester Square, gathered some girls round her, girls who had known her in the days of her dissipation, and reminding them of her drunken condition the last time they had seen her, she told them how God was making her spoiled life good, and pleaded with them to follow her example. A few days after," says Sister Margaret, " she came to see me, and told me of the wonderful change God had made in her life."

This is only one story of the many that might be told.

As I sat in that room and thought of the miracles of Grace it had witnessed, of the frightened young girls who had found it a haven of refuge, and of the broken-hearted mothers who had come in the hope of finding their daughters, and not always in vain : and as I listened to instance after instance of the adroit and persistent methods Sister Margaret had used to see the wrong righted, without scandal or bitterness, and yet with unflinching purpose, my heart rejoiced at such a bit of work carried on throughout the years. Meyer was behind it all. When I asked that brave woman whether she liked living in the slums she answered, "I wouldn't live anywhere else in the world."

Take this for another story. "On Christmas Day, 1919, I had a Christmas supper. I laid the table and put a small present for whomsoever might come in. Then I went out to seek my guests. Between midnight and one o'clock I could find no one. Returning home, I put some finishing touches on the table and had a little more prayer, telling my Master that the guests must be His choice, not mine.

"So again I went out, and this time I found ten poor derelicts, all more or less under the influence of drink. As I looked round the table I felt that they were not my choice but they were certainly *His*, and I asked that I might have a share of His love and pity. Our party began at 2.30 a.m. and finished about 5.30. We talked about other Christmasses when we were children, and how they had got down to this Christmas.

"*Out of the ten who came, eight have now left the streets and are working hard to get right.* His Name is rightly called Jesus, for He shall save His people from their sins."

*   *   *   *   *

But warning and rescue are not sufficient. There remains the care of the unwanted child to complete the work, and under the guidance of God Dr. Meyer also put his hand to this bit of philanthropy. It has been computed that twenty-five thousand homeless babes are born every year in the British Isles. It is one of the unexplained mysteries of life why, when the whole population has freedom of action, the number of illegitimate births should scarcely vary year by year.

Dr. Meyer, with others, for years had given support to an effort to care for these children, but it came to an end through financial embarrassment. But when Miss Hames and Mr. Beesley called a few friends together and urged that a new attempt should be made to extend a helping hand to heart-broken girl-mothers, to revive hope and new courage in their breasts and to place their feet on firm ground, Dr. Meyer declared it to be the call of God. There and then he, with the Rev. John Bradford, Mr. Robert Caldwell, Miss Caroline Mary Hames and Mr. Beesley, consecrated themselves to the work, and the initial steps were taken to establish what is now known under the descriptive but somewhat unwieldy title of " Homeless Children's Aid and Adoption Society," to which was afterwards added, " and F. B. Meyer's Children's Home," and a third interpreting line, " Society for Befriending the Unmarried Mother and Child."

More than two thousand children have been befriended and about a thousand have been adopted into suitable homes, amongst them the boy a month old who was left in a Gladstone bag on the doorsteps of the offices in Westminster Bridge Road on Dr. Meyer's birthday, April, 1926, and afterwards dedicated to God in Christ Church under the name of Frederick Poole Hawkstone.

The Children's Home is at Leytonstone. It remains as one of his memorials, and will no doubt continue to be supported in its Christ-like service.

CHAPTER SIXTEEN

His Last Captaincy

WHETHER Dr. Meyer originated a movement or joined in a movement, it seemed inevitable that he should be its leader. This was not a rule without an exception, for he was, for instance, associated with Dr. Paton of Nottingham in the Lingfield Farm Colony from its inception. He became President of a score of societies in his time, many of them noted in previous chapters. When he worked with others he was more apt to say, " Who will join me " than " Let us." Like Gladstone, he was prepared to be leader because his eyes were on the goal, and he knew he could guide to it, while, with all respect, he was not quite so sure of other people. And other people recognised his driving power and were glad to follow his lead.

He could truly say, " I live, yet not I, but Christ liveth in me " ; no man more really denied self and exalted the Lord Jesus, and if sometimes, though the objective " I " was denied, the subjective " Me " obtruded itself, it was the egotism not of a self-seeker but of a child.

Dr. Parker once said of him, " Here is my friend, Mr. Meyer. He always has a new scheme—the sweetest and brightest thing ever seen in the market-place. He calls upon me before nine o'clock in the morning, having risen a great while before then, and he always gets younger and younger. He is to me a most welcome visitor : he brings a benediction with him, a better air than earth's poor murky climate, and he never leaves me without the impression that I have been face to face with a man of God."

As a close friend of Dr. Grattan Guinness, in his early
ministry it was natural that he should be deeply interested
in the Second Advent of Christ, and quite as natural that he
should sympathise with the historical interpretation of the
Book of Revelation, to which I believe he still inclined at
the end of his life. But when, in view of two facts, first,
that the early Church thought that Christ's Epiphany was
imminent, and second, that the history of the Church is
lost in obscurity at the end of the first century, Mr. E.
Hampden Cook propounded the view that little is said about
the saints of those days, because Christ's promise was
fulfilled, and the saints alive on earth toward the end of the
century were rapt to heaven according to His word,
Mr. Meyer said, " In the main I thoroughly accept your
conclusion. It must be true." The theory is not so fantastic
as it seems, and Mr. Cook gave cogent reasons for his faith—
a faith which would at once justify the hope of the early
Christians, and account in great measure, by the miracle
it involved, for the rapid spread of Christianity in the next
century. That there is no record of the event he argued is
justified by the fact that there was nobody left to record it.

On the first day of 1905 Mr. Meyer preached a sermon
advocating this view, which attracted considerable attention, one of the London daily newspapers giving an
extended report of it. How long he held the view is not
known, but Mr. Alfred Ellis of Amersham tells me that
when he came to open the Church there he found him in
the vestry with his Bible open at the Thessalonian Epistles,
and he said that he wished he knew the meaning of the
verse about being caught up in the air, to which Mr. Ellis
as a practical lawyer, replied, " Why not believe that it
means what it says ? " and Dr. Meyer gave a glad response.
It was not always easy to know when he asked questions
of that sort, whether he was giving a test or giving a
testimony.

At any rate, in later years he became very pronounced
on the subject. Rev. E. L. Langston, of Sevenoaks, knowing
the matter from the beginning, has been good enough to

give the following details concerning the formation of the Advent Testimony Movement :—

" It came about as follows. On November 2nd, 1917, every student of prophecy was thrilled at the announcement that the then Mr. Balfour had written to Lord Rothschild in the name of the British Government stating that they were prepared to give facilities for the Jews to settle in Palestine and make it their national home.

" The late Rev. Alfred Bird immediately got into touch with Dr. Meyer and urged him to start some movement to bring home to the Christian public the significance of this remarkable edict. Dr. Meyer then communicated with Dr. Alfred Burton and myself, then officials of the Prophecy Investigation Society, and then we got into touch with Dr. Campbell Morgan, Dr. J. Stuart Holden, Prebendary F. S Webster, Prebendary H. M. Webb-Peploe and Prebendary H. E. Fox. We met together and drew up a basis for the formation of the Advent Testimony and Preparation Movement.

" Our first meetings were held at Queen's Hall, in December, 1917, and they were simply magnificent. Bible readings and addresses, morning, afternoon, and evening, were given by the founders of this new movement. The Queen's Hall was far too small to accommodate all that wished to attend throughout the day. Ever since then, the movement has held monthly meetings either at the Queen's Hall or at the Kingsway Hall, and as a result of these gatherings branches have been formed all over the country, in America, in Australia, and many parts of the Mission Field.

" It is a constant amazement to us how magnificently our meetings are supported and what power and enthusiasm there always is at our gatherings. We feel we have been called by God to prepare the way for the coming again of the Lord Jesus Christ.

" The great personality during the past twelve years behind this movement has undoubtedly been our late President, Dr. F. B. Meyer. Students of prophecy are liable

to disagree as to details of interpretation, but the striking
testimony of our platform is its remarkable unity. This
also is due in large measure to the magnificent spiritual
leadership of our late revered friend. We miss him sorely."

Mr. Langston, himself an ardent herald of the Coming
Day, says quite truly that expounders of prophecy are
liable to disagree in details, but surely it might be taken for
granted that all those who so frequently pray " Thy
Kingdom come " should expect an answer to their prayer.
All expect Christ to come. The main difference between
Christians is that some expect the Kingdom to come before
the King and others expect the King to come before the
Kingdom. Amongst the latter Dr. Meyer ranged himself
without hesitation, and though the Great War was not the
Midnight Cry, as he and some others suggested, he held
fast to his hope to the end, and did much, in this and in
other countries, to hearten believers with the thought of
our Lord's speedy advent. The method of Christ's approach
is very important, but it is secondary. The main thing is
that we expect His reign on earth.

Miss Christabel Pankhurst, to the surprise of those who
only knew her as a militant Suffragist, has also become an
eloquent exponent of the need, and the hope, of Christ's
Return to the world for which He died, all other hope being
in vain. First aroused to the thought of it by the title of
Dr. Grattan Guinness's great book, " The Approaching End
of the Age," she has studied and written and spoken much
on the subject. Early in her advocacy she came into touch
with Dr. Meyer and joined him in meetings in various parts
of the country—meetings, which it is hardly necessary to
say, were very crowded. The combination of two such
personalities, apart altogether from the subject, made a
strong appeal. She has kindly written, with a good deal of
insight, the following most discriminating estimate of
Dr. Meyer, based on her brief acquaintance with him :—

" My conversations with Dr. Meyer were always of our
Father's business. He was a fount of wisdom and good
counsel, as you know, and was always willing to advise and

encourage others in their Christian service. By name
Dr. Meyer was, of course, always well known to me, as to
every one, but I had never met him until my return from the
United States and Canada some years ago.

" In 1918 I first became interested in prophecy, but did
not then realise Dr. Meyer's position with regard to it, as
when he and others issued their historic manifesto and held
the first Queen's Hall meeting I was abroad on war work,
and so did not see any newspaper report of the launching of
the A.T.P.M. At a later date, and on the eve of sailing for
America, I saw an announcement of the A.T.P.M. meetings
at Kingsway Hall, and there heard Dr. Meyer and others
speak. While in America I wrote to Dr. Meyer as leader of
the A.T.P.M. and told him of my interest in, and agreement
with, the movement, and incidentally informed him that I
was writing a book (" The Lord Cometh ") at the invitation
of an American publisher.

" We continued our correspondence from time to time,
and on my return to England I met Dr. Meyer for the first
time. He wanted me to speak in various centres and I did so.
Every now and then, during three years or so, we have met
periodically, and always I have been impressed, and
increasingly so, by his wonderful serenity and glowing
saintliness, his intense concentration on his Master's service,
his selfless interest in the efforts of others, his noble and
dignified humility of spirit which raised him to so high a
level and gave him so much authority. He was truly a
leader of others and a father in God, to all of less experience
and shorter service.

" In the last year and even months of his life I thought
that he gained very definitely in power and spiritual insight.
At a conference which he summoned I was present, and it
seemed to me our Lord had revealed to him some new height
and depth and given him further lessons to be imparted to
others.

" Of late I have been re-reading his little booklets, and
surely it may be said that he being dead yet speaketh.
I believe that his writings will be used by God more power-

fully and fruitfully than ever, since the writer's departure, and that his own prayers will be answered beyond anything that even he asked or thought.

" Within a few days of his death I had two notes from him expressing his satisfaction with my new book, and breathing all his usual confidence and encouragement." When I asked Miss Pankhurst what she thought of Dr. Meyer, without hesitation she answered, " He was a Napoleon."

The outshining of Christ's glory and the revealing of the sons of God, is the goal towards which the whole creation moves—moves not without guidance nor without certainty. The watchword of the early followers of Christ, as glad eyes looked into glad eyes, should be ours—" Maranatha ! " In France, when Napoleon was in Elba, a great longing rose in the hearts of many people that he should come back again. They dared not openly speak their purpose, but they chose as their sign the violet. They hoped their winter would soon be past, the violet was the token of the spring. They wore violets in their dress, and their greeting when they met kindred spirits was " *Aimez-vous la violette* ? " In saying that they said nothing and they said everything. Those who loved the violet were looking for the return of the Great Victor. They did not know how he would come, but it was he, and none other, they desired ; they differed in a thousand ways, but if they declared they loved the violet, they possessed the password to each other's hearts. Their hero came at length, only, alas, to lead them to Waterloo, and himself to the lonely vigil in St. Helena. When our Great Captain returns it will be His eternal triumph. *Aimez-vous la violette ?*

As one by one His soldiers fall, we cry, " Come quickly, Lord Jesus ! Make Thy Presence known ! Appear to our joy ! " and if F. B. Meyer could speak again to us, he might voice his assurance in words of Scripture, whose first use had another meaning. " As I live, saith the King whose name is the Lord of Hosts, surely as Tabor is among the mountains and Carmel by the sea, so shall He come."

CHAPTER SEVENTEEN

Two Notable Occasions

AMONG the many great gatherings at Christ Church two stand out as specially memorable. The first, Dr. Meyer's Ministerial Jubilee on June 30th, 1920 : the second, the Celebration of his Eightieth Birthday on April 8th, 1927. To few men is it given to minister the Word of God for half a century, to fewer still to be still preaching at the age of fourscore. Dr. Meyer had the double honour.

In addition to himself and Dr. W. C. Poole his colleague and successor, the only speaker who gave greeting at both meetings was Dr. Dinsdale Young, his neighbour on the other side of the river, who was always ready to come to his help. On both occasions Christ Church was crowded by enthusiastic friends, twice in the first meeting the congregation rose and cheered, and once in the second : an evidence of very strong feeling in such a stately sanctuary. On both evenings they cheered when Dr. Meyer rose to reply, on the first when Sir Alfred Pearce Gould, his old friend, turned to him and clasping his hand said, " It is not usual, nay, it is rare for men to use to one another words such as these, which I sincerely believe express what we all feel. Dear Dr. Meyer, we love you ! We love you ! "

The Archbishop of Canterbury, himself only a year younger than Dr. Meyer, sent a cordial message to both meetings. At the first the other speakers were Dr. J. Stuart Holden, who acknowledged his personal obligation to Dr. Meyer : and Dr. J. H. Jowett, who played upon the taut strings until the air was full of thanksgiving for the man who, through fifty years, had pointed his fellows to

Christ, and constrained them by the winsomeness of his pure passion to His glorious service. He reminded Dr. Meyer that Mr. Gladstone was but beginning his third volume when he was the same age, and told how, long ago, Mr. Meyer had looked into a mirror and said to himself, " That face won't do : it wants lighting up," and it was lit up and kept lighted.

On the second occasion there were five-minute speeches on Dr. Meyer's life—" The Gladness of Spring," " The Glory of Summer," " The Fulfilment of Autumn," " The Promise of Winter "—the speakers being Rev. Alfred J. Kaye, Rev. W. Y. Fullerton, Rev. H. Tydeman Chilvers and Dr. John Wilson. It was announced by Pastor Findlay that the circulation of Dr. Meyer's books, large and small, by one firm alone was 2,545,000.

Then Mr. B. A. Glanvill presented him with a cheque for £800 as a token of the esteem of hundreds of friends ; Rev. E. L. Langston, who had spoken earlier in the evening, asked his acceptance of £50 from friends of the Second Advent and Testimony Movement. Then Mr. Looker, who had at the Jubilee Meeting made the presentation of £750, at this meeting gave Dr. Meyer a portable wireless set ; which, being set in motion as it was presented, sent out a music-hall ditty, until it was hurriedly hushed. In future days it gave him great joy to turn on the music when he was visiting children's or old people's gatherings.

On each occasion Dr. Meyer was just himself as he rose to reply. Affection beamed on him from thousands of eyes in the congregation, heads nodded, handkerchiefs wiped furtive tears from eyes. In ringing tones the old man eloquently closed his second speech with the homely words, " I'll have another go," and the Hallelujah Chorus ended the Day of Praise.

The next day Dr. Meyer had the exquisite pleasure of apportioning his gifts from the presentation of the previous evening. As an evidence of his generous spirit, and the width of his sympathy, a list of his benefactions may be given. To Christ Church, £420 ; Three gifts for Social Service, £100 ; Sunday Schools, £30 ; Institute, £5 ; Cripples' Parlour, £5 ; Miss Sharman's Orphan Home, £5 ; Walworth Creche, £2 ; F. B. Meyer's Children's Home, £50.

Ten guineas each to the Religious Tract Society, The Bible Society, China Inland Mission, Baptist Missionary Society, London Missionary Society, Sunday Defence League. £88 to The Regions Beyond Missionary Union, etc.

Five guineas each to Dr. Barnardo's Homes, National Children's Homes, World's Sunday School Association, National Sunday School Union, Christian Endeavour Union. Three guineas to the Brotherhood Federation. Two guineas to the Evangelical Alliance.

These amounts with others left ten shillings still in hand. Then he remembered that he ought to have given something to the Spanish Gospel Mission and to the Alliance of Honour, and he sent them both a donation, glad to do the extra thing.

To the *London Evening News* he contributed a lengthy article, " Thoughts at 80," written on his birthday. " I must confess myself a confirmed optimist : only eager that my fellow-countrymen may prove themselves to be worthy to be the heirs and pioneers of that good time coming, which has been the dream of the ages.

" We may differ widely as to the methods by which this vision of a New Heaven on Earth may be realised. Whether that method is to be Apocalyptic or gradual, by instantaneous or protracted processes need not for the moment divide us."

In the *Sunday Express* of London, a year later, another article from his pen, " My Religion—at 81," aroused much attention. " Probably it would have been easier to state my religious faith and outlook when I was eighteen than now when the figures are reversed. But knowing all that I know of the travail, the agony, and the heart-break ; behind it all, through it all, dealing with it all—*God is Love*.

" Whatever else the facts and doctrine of the Incarnation

and the Death on the Cross stand for, they reveal a yearning love in the Unseen, and on the part of the Divine Being, which is reflected in the mother's love for her suffering child. So have we seen the whole sun reflected in a dewdrop.

" ' What ugly hands you have, mother,' said a child as she sat on her mother's knee. ' Yes,' was the reply, ' but they were not like that before you fell into the fire, and mother's hands got burned in saving you.'

" The intrusion of God, in the Person of Christ, into our nature and world, leads me to expect a Second Advent when Love will again be manifested in His overcoming and perfected Victory.

" The moral of all this is—receive and pass on ! Touch God on the one hand and man on the other ! Let the River of Life have vent through your life. Receive and give ! "

To be fitted for this life he laid emphasis on morning prayer and the method he recommended to others, and practised himself, was Eightfold : 1. Approach to God with reverence. 2. Adoration. 3. Confession. 4. The Child's Uplook into the Father's face. 5. Communion. 6. Forecast of future hours, reception of grace sufficient for the coming day. 7. Pleading of promises for objects and especial guidance. 8. Intercessions, not only for dear ones but for Missionaries, Wanderers, those stricken, those fallen, and for the Speedy Advent of the Kingdom of our Lord.

CHAPTER EIGHTEEN

A Boy Again

Speaking at a Young Life Campaign Meeting at Kingsway Hall in May, 1928, Dr. Meyer said, " They talk about a man getting back to his second childhood. I am getting back to my second boyhood " : and then he went on to tell a story about somebody else and then a bit about himself. In it all he spoke to those young people with the candour and naïveté of youth. Early in his youth he naturally and spontaneously thought and spoke of the Lord Jesus Christ : later he was much occupied with the thought and presence of the Holy Spirit : towards the end he as naturally and spontaneously turned to the Father. He was a boy again.

" When I was in Denmark," he said, " I found that my translator was ill and I had a man who did not understand very much English, though he knew a lot of Danish, and I was extremely anxious that my meetings there should be crowned with blessing. As we were sitting at dinner, the present Lord Radstock happened to have come from Norway, and I remember so well he was sitting opposite to me, and he told this story :—

" ' I was staying in one of the nicest hotels in Norway, crowded with a number of people who had come there for rest and change, but everything was spoiled by a little girl who was beginning to learn music and insisted upon coming into the drawing room whenever she chose and starting upon the piano with one finger and one note and one discord every time, and whenever people saw this child arrive and make for that piano everybody bolted into the open air and left the child mistress of all she surveyed. Presently one of

the finest musicians in Norway, on his wedding tour, came
there and took in the situation, and instead of vanishing
when the other people vanished, he took a stool and sat
beside the child at the piano, and for every note that she
struck he struck the most exquisite chord of music ; and
she struck another note and another note and another note,
and all the time he kept introducing a most lovely accom-
paniment ; and the notes floated outside and the people
for the first time heard music from that piano and streamed
back. The child went on strumming and the man went on
with his accompanying chords, and when the child came to
a more terrible mistake than usual he improvised a finer
outburst of music ; and so it went on for twenty minutes,
and then he took the child by the hand and led her round
the company that sat there listening and said : " Ladies
and Gentlemen, I want to introduce to you the young lady
to whom you are indebted for the music of this afternoon."
The child knew well enough that she had not done it, but
everybody there paid their compliments and thanks to him.'

" I cannot tell you what that story was to me, nor can
I tell you how all through the years it has helped me. I have
been that child at the piano of God's truth, I have tried my
level best to make music with my one finger, and again and
again and again I have come away feeling that there has
been some terrible failure and discord ; but, oh, I have
also found the Holy Spirit sitting by my side, and for
every note of discord I have made He has struck a nobler
note. I hope you will never forget this story, and when
you are in that Sunday School or in that Open Air, or
trying to speak to a lad or a girl about God, and you feel
that you are only making mistakes and failures and false
notes, believe that the blessed Holy Spirit is by your side
and is turning your discords and your poor piano notes into
the Hallelujah Chorus.

" If you will turn to Acts, Chapters xiv and xv, you will
find two wonderful prepositions of the work of the Holy
Ghost. If you know your Greek, one is *dia*, ' through,' and
the other is *meta*, ' with.' These two prepositions are applied

to the Holy Spirit. How wonderful to think that even He speaks *through* you, and how He works *with* you. Again and again when I have been preaching to congregations and have felt that I was doing poor work, I said to Him, ' Great Partner, things have gone to pieces my end, put an extra pressure on Thine.' When you and the Holy Spirit are in partnership and you feel you are making such a mistake, and you don't know how to begin or how to end, and you feel sometimes confused and disappointed, you just say, ' Great Partner, I cannot see you, but open the piano of this soul, lay Thy hand upon it, and make sweet music which will start the soul upon a new and higher level.'

" Now the other little bit is about myself, and of course when a man gets to be eighty-one he can talk about himself. Well, of course I would not do it if I were in a grown-up audience—I'm scared of old people—but I don't mind talking to you, because you are different and you and I are on a level. Well now (this is a bit of biography), when I was fifty, some thirty-one years ago, I was going down to my church and was crossing over the parade ground behind the Horse Guards, and I looked up to Christ and I said, ' Lord, give me an uplifting text,' and He said, ' He that believeth in Me, out of him shall flow rivers of living water, as the Scripture hath said.' And He said, ' I am going to fulfil that in you, and out of your life there are to flow rivers of living water.' And I said, ' Lord Jesus, it isn't in me, but if You like to let it flow through me, it will be good.'

" Well, I could not think for the moment what that text meant, so I started looking into the Bible, and of course, there is no other passage that really meets the case except that in Ezekiel, about the river that started like a little struggling stream, came first to the ankles, then grew to the knees, and then grew to the loins and to the heart, and then to waters to swim in.

" Now I can swim all right (I really can). When I took a lot of my young fellows, years ago now, to Wales (I was a new parson, and I don't think they thought I was up to sample), there was a long raft going out into the water and a deep dive from it, and I was the only one who dared to take the dive, and ever after that they respected me. Therefore, you see I do know what swimming is.

" I saw that if I were to swim out to save men and women who were drowning, three things must happen. First to my feet, my ankles—I must walk in God's way. Then the water had to come to my knees—I had to learn to pray. Then to the loins—I had to keep my body under. And so the ankles and the knees and the heart and the loins are kept absolutely pure and sweet by Jesus, and then it is that we can swim, we can save other people who are drifting down to perdition : those three conditions make it possible for God to do His saving work through human lives."

The Rev. F. A. Robinson of Toronto tells of his fellowship with him in Canada in these latter years ; some of the incidents he has written for the *Sunday School Times*, that great American journal, some he has given in a private letter :—

" During one of our quiet chats on his last tour, he said, ' I do hope my Father will let the river of my life go flowing fully till the finish. I don't want it to end in a swamp.'

" Sometimes he could not avoid the demonstrations that love prompted. On one such occasion he prayed, ' The people are going to make a fuss over me in trying to make me happy. Oh, my Lord, won't you give me something that will make me a more useful man to help them ? '

" A telegram needed great care in wording. I suggested a slight change. ' Yes, I think that would be better,' and in handing the telegram back to me for sending, he added, ' Father, we thank Thee for helping us to say the right thing : we leave all the rest to Thy loving control.' And he did.

" I see that earnest face radiant with memories of what God wrought because he was not disobedient to the heavenly vision. I see the aged preacher bending forward in the high-backed chair which a friend persuaded him to use in his late ministry. He looks at a group of young men near the pulpit. He rises to his feet a moment, and appealingly cries, ' Oh, my dear young brothers, the partnership of Christ is very wonderful. He does a deep work in your heart and then suddenly He opens a door. It may be a tiny door, just a little ajar, but you push it, and that tiny door opens into a large room, that opens into a still larger room, and so on. That is how life with Him goes on.'

" Once after a slight misunderstanding with a certain man, I referred to the fact that I had been wondering if God was laughing, and saying, ' Those funny children of Mine down there ! ' ' Did you really think that ? ' he replied. ' Last night, after I left you, I went to bed and laughed until I was exhausted. I looked up and said, " Oh, Lord, the people say I am a dear old saint, and here all this has been going on. Isn't it funny, Lord ? " ' There was the boy.

" On the morning of August 31st, 1927, he was to arrive in Montreal at Bonaventure Station. Careful instructions had been written him. I had gone to that city on an early train and had breakfast with friends. We ordered a taxi to be at the house by the end of the meal as we had not much time to spare. On the way down, for no earthly reason (note the adjective) I suggested that it might be wise to drive to the Windsor Station, Canadian Pacific Railway, and I would meet the train coming over that line, even though I expected Dr. Meyer at the other station. It was agreed that my friend should go down to the Canadian National Railway Station, where the train we had indicated was to arrive. Just as I was stepping out of the car I could see over the heads of the crowd Dr. Meyer getting into another taxi. I hurried to him and he looked as if he had just dropped out of heaven. As we drove along he said quietly, ' I knew there had been a bungle and that I had been put into the wrong train, so I told God about it, and said, " Please, Father, let Mr. Robinson meet me in Montreal," and I knew it would be all right. Oh ! God is so good, so good, my friend.' "

His friend, the Rev. E. Palgrave Davy, tells of a visit to

his home when, after lunch, he said he must just have twenty minutes sleep before going to a meeting. " I was travelling much of the night, coming from the North, and I need a little rest."

" All right," said his friend, " you go and lie down and I will come in and waken you in half an hour."

" Oh, no ! " he replied. " You mustn't do that. The Lord always wakes me up just when I ask Him. I say to Him, ' Lord, Thou knowest Thy child is tired and needs rest, and I have a meeting to address. Please give me a little sleep and wake me in twenty minutes ' ; and He always does, whatever time I ask Him. Oh, no : I mustn't let you waken me. That would seem as though I didn't trust Him."

And sure enough he appeared in less than half an hour.

A brother minister tells me that when Dr. Meyer was a guest in his home he gathered the children round him and interested them in showing them his keys. They remember one specially. " That was my father's key," he said, " the key to the place where he kept his treasures." Then he said, pointing upward, " You know your Father has given you His key. I hope you will make use of it, for it opens to you all His treasures of goodness and help." The eldest boy replied, " Yes, I will," and from that day he has been seeking to fit himself to be a missionary, never wavering in his purpose—he is using his Father's Key. The boy appealed to the boy.

CHAPTER NINETEEN

A COMPOSITE PICTURE

THE following records of the impressions made on three competent observers, if merged as in a composite photograph, will give a realistic picture of the man, apart from the things in his personality which were merely accidental and adventitious.

In a lengthy article in *Great Thoughts* for January, 1904, Mr. Raymond Blathwayt, the well-known journalist, shows a great deal of insight into the moving springs of Dr. Meyer's life.

" Most people who know Mr. Meyer would have no hesitation in writing him down a convinced optimist, ever seeing the bright side of everything, ever hopeful, ever vigorous, ever confident of the ultimate triumph of good over evil. And they would be right. He is delightfully hopeful and inspiring, his whole record is one of brilliant effort, of marvellous achievement, but he is far too keen, far too thoughtful a man, he is infinitely too great a student of humanity, and in himself he is immeasurably too human, not to be overcome now and again by the pessimistic views of life which must overtake a man engaged, as he has been, in working amidst the most terrible surroundings that it is possible for a man to work. He has gone down into the very depths of human despair, he has confronted men and women in whom all appearance of even humanity has been lost for ever, he has seen too often and too clearly the seamy side of human nature, not to be sad and pessimistic now and then.

" And curiously enough the thing that most impressed me on the recent occasions when I have met and talked with him—for hours at a time—was this very tendency to pessimism ; a very gentle pessimism, a pessimism undemonstrative and unaggressive, but still pessimism decided, well thought out, scientifically reasoned and accounted for, for all that. To the ordinary casual observer and acquaintance this statement will probably appear absurd. ' Oh ! ' I can hear such an one declaring, ' how ridiculous ! Why it's the very reverse. Meyer is one of the most cheery men it is possible to conceive.' Which is just where they are right, and just where they are wrong. In certain respects, though full of a brilliant and life-compelling faith ; a worker of almost feverish earnestness, with, in many respects, a keen, vivid and thoroughly sane and healthy outlook upon life, Mr. Meyer is one who has the courage of his convictions and he reads the signs of the times as they appear to him actually to portend. With the almost inevitable result that he takes a somewhat sad and pessimistic view of the present and future of the body politic generally

" He does not consider that the present day makes for the righteousness of the community as a whole or that humanity in the mass is on the upward path.

" Whilst fully conscious of the increased earnestness of the age in many respects, he recognises more keenly still that the hostile influences are more vigorously vibrant and vital than ever they were before. Scepticism, immorality to an appalling extent, absolute and entire indifference to all religious teaching, the total absence of ideals, the growing materialism of the day, the utter disregard of the things of the spirit world ; all these things he regards, massed as a hostile army, against the striving after a higher and a better life which is still characteristic of a noble-hearted minority. But still it is a minority and this is where his sadness and his pessimism comes in. He gives me that idea of a man weighed down by the burden of a world grown old in sin and enfeebled by premature decay.

" And all the while he himself is so absolutely the

reverse. Of all our religious workers he is, in certain respects, the most inspiring, the most hope-compelling that I have ever known ; for you are not to imagine for a single second that he ever allows this pessimism of his to impede his work for humanity, or that it stands in the way of all his self-sacrificing efforts on behalf of the sin-laden, diseased and destitute waifs and wastrels of our great city. Not a bit of it. The man who more than any one I have ever met, perhaps, except Father Dolling, has realised the brotherhood of man in its entirety, is the last person in the world to relax efforts or to abandon hope on behalf of those to whom he has given up his whole hard-working and devoted life.

" I give but my own personal idea of him, I do but lift the veil for a moment, and I do so because I cannot help realising that in a wise pessimism lies often the secret of great self-sacrifice and high achievement. Optimism, as I have just said, is often selfish, frequently shallow, almost always short-sighted. The pessimist who is not overcome by his pessimism or whose hands are not stayed by his outlook on life is frequently enough he who accomplishes most enduring and finest work in the end. And such a man is F. B. Meyer.

" And he is neither sugary nor sentimental. That is a popular misunderstanding which has somehow or another gathered round about Mr. Meyer, and which I cannot too emphatically contradict. Meyer is a remarkably thoughtful and an extremely well read man, though I do not suppose he would make any claim whatever to deep or wide scholarship, any more than I should make such claim on his behalf. He is a much travelled man, who has turned his travels to the best mental purpose ; he is a great student of human nature ; he knows much of humanity, and knowing much, he is able to make great allowances for its frailties and faults, but he is an unsparing denunciator of sin ; swift, scathing, direct ; pitying the sinner, he is boundless in his indignation against, and his contempt for, the sin. It will easily be imagined, therefore, that he is a preacher who appeals to many very widely differing sections of the community.

" ' The truth of the matter is,' he said, ' and you may say what you like, the human heart cannot exist without God and some kind of belief in a future life. Materialism cannot satisfy the soul of man for ever and ever. It never has done so in the history of the world and I am quite sure it never will. And this becomes increasingly manifest amongst the manliest lives. Let a Moody go through the American continent, and let him preach in the great mining or lumber camps where men live the lives of primal man, and they flock to hear him and fall like shocks of wheat before the Gospel stroke.

" ' It is the men of little, narrow, circumscribed lives, the men who pass their safe, timid little existences between the walls of a great city, and who know little or nothing of the danger and peril of life outside, that become sceptics and atheists—though I am one who denies the existence of a real genuine atheist. Remember this, men can't do without religion. If there is an ebb, there is a tide ; if there is a recess, there is a flow.'

" These are the words, are they not, of a strong man. Mr. Meyer's views of religion are those of a man who has toiled and suffered, not so much for himself as for others, which is mainly where his strength comes in."

The characterisation by the Rev. W. H. Bocock of Flatbush, New York State, is a balanced judgment which commends itself as substantially accurate.

" Probably Frederick B. Meyer is not to all men what he is to the writer. *Tot homines, tot mentes.* His manner of conceiving and expressing truth in his devotional writings may not appeal to all. But I have yet to meet one who has listened to his earnest and searching words without being deeply moved. No one can deny that he is a man of exceptional power.

" Never shall I forget the first sermon I heard him preach. It was at Northfield. We had been listening for a week to other men known throughout the land as men of piety, understanding of the Scriptures, and success in Christian work. But people who had listened to him the summer before kept saying, ' Wait till Meyer comes.' At the beginning of the second week he came.

" Expectation had been so aroused that we were prepared to be disappointed. And truly his appearance as he sat upon the platform was disappointing. Slender and fragile in build, bent over at that time with lumbago, with a small head and face peaked and thin, he seemed, except for the shining of his countenance, completely destitute of those outward graces which command the eye and are half the battle to a speaker. But all thought of disappointment fled when he began to speak. In a voice, not strong, but clear, sympathetic, penetrating, he announced a text which I did not remember to have seen, ' They that receive abundance of grace shall reign in life.' The royal life of conquest over self—how beautiful and winsome the ideal became under his graphic touch ! How faithfully he dealt with his hearers, flashing the searchlight of God's purifying truth into many dark corners of the heart and shaming us because of our carnality. At its conclusion we felt dazed, as though we had seen some unaccustomed sight—the sight of ourselves as we really were and the sight of ourselves as God would have us be.

" The impression thus produced by his first sermon was deepened and intensified as, during the week following, he spoke to us from such texts and themes as, ' Wherefore, O King Agrippa, I was not disobedient to the heavenly vision,' ' The Potter and the Clay,' ' The Spirit overcoming the flesh,' ' Married to another,' ' The Pentecostal gift,' ' Fellowship with Christ.' We had many times listened to men who had handed us truth across the counter of their personality, but here was a man who drew up truth, clear, fresh and satisfying, out of the deep well of his own personal experience. We heard not simply texts and their exposition, but we were allowed to see the workings of a living soul under the healing touches of God's Spirit, and the truth reached us with a recommendation from a life which could not be mistaken. His words, therefore, were authoritative ; every tone and accent of his speech rang true. Was it strange that the entire convention received a marked spiritual uplift ? Surely here was power of a high order.

" Not always is a man on his native heath what he is on foreign soil. Dr. John Hall once called attention to the well-known fact that certain brilliant pulpiteers, who supply churches for short periods and who captivate by their eloquence, are sometimes a kind of pianette with a limited number of tunes, rather than Eolian harps from whose strings the free winds of heaven evoke music. Mr. Meyer is of the latter rather than the former order.

" But others are men of power. Power of any kind is attractive and compelling. Many preachers in London and elsewhere draw large audiences, but I would call attention to the leading quality of Mr. Meyer's power. It is mainly spiritual. Let me compare or contrast in one particular the preaching of F. W. Farrar and F. B. Meyer. It was my good fortune to hear Dean Farrar in Westminister Abbey on ' Enthusiasm.' The Editor of *The Outlook*, commenting on this sermon in its columns, spoke of it as one of the three great sermons he heard in Great Britain. And indeed it was great in the highest sense of the word. It was in Dean Farrar's best vein. It was the product of ripe scholarship, interfused by the divine enthusiasm with which it dealt ; and it revealed the historical research, the rhetorical grace and power, and the noble spiritual and ethical temper characteristic of the speaker. It dazzled while it warmed It was powerful, but the elements of its power were many. None but Dean Farrar could have done it.

" The following Thursday morning I heard Mr. Meyer, and, strangely enough, on a similar theme—' The Lamp and the Furnace.' The material of the sermon was comparatively slender, gathered mainly from the context, but it was on fire. The sermon itself was a lamp and a furnace— light and heat. The simplicity, directness, calm intensity, and a peculiarly wistful element in the speaker's utterance, brought it home, and in the hush of the immense church one felt that the Spirit of God was dealing with the souls of the listeners. There is a difference easily felt between the quiet of admiring interest and the deep calm of spiritual introspection. I may have been mistaken, but I felt that with a slighter equipment of rhetoric and scholarship Mr. Meyer was producing a deeper and more lasting effect.

"What, then, is the secret of his unusual power? I have anticipated the answer We find it, I think, in his consecration.

"What is the secret of any preacher's power? It is folly to seek it in any single thing. Power is not generated by tricks of voice or gesture or style, but it wells up out of the life. The sources of all pulpit power are twofold— personality and spirituality. By personality we mean what a man is by natural endowment and education, by heredity and environment. Spirituality is the power which is added when the personality of the man is linked to the personality of God, when what the man is is completed by what God is. The measure of any Christian worker's power will depend on the fulness and richness of his personality, and the entirety of his consecration. With equal consecration the man of greater natural force will do the larger work. But the man of less original power, but greater consecration, will excel his more gifted brother in spiritual usefulness.

"The power of Mr. Meyer has its source in his spirituality rather than in his personality, though the two cannot be thus separated except for clearness of thought. He is a conduit rather than an original fountain. To the outward view certainly he is not indebted to nature more than the average man. And just because of this he is a most encouraging character to study. One feels in meeting and hearing him, perhaps mistakenly, that he himself is fitted by nature to do as well.

"If his force resided in great physical or magnetic power he would discourage men of weaker frame. Fowler and Wells said of Henry Ward Beecher, ' He is a magnificent animal,' and Mr. Beecher has himself told how in moments of inspiration he has felt his heart-pump fairly lashing the blood up into his brain. A man of such vitality cannot help being great, we say, and feel no particular incentive from his example. But physical vitality does not figure as an important element in Mr. Meyer's power. Not that he is wanting in bodily strength, but that he is no better off in this respect, if so well off, as the average man.

"Nor is he a man of exceptional intellectual power. In this, too, there is incentive and encouragement. We decline to accept his own modest estimate of himself. 'I am,' said he, 'a man of two talents.' His sermons and addresses are not marked by that intellectual quality which is so conspicuous in the sermons of F. W. Robertson and Philips Brooks. Of this, however, he is not destitute. Occasional paragraphs will disclose profound and discriminating thinking, but power of mentality is not characteristic of him above other intelligent and educated men.

"Nor is his attractiveness to be found mainly in the charm of style or utterance, though in both he has peculiar excellence. I have already alluded to his manner of speaking. His language is a clear and transparent medium for his thought. His illustrations are graphic and luminous, and often a sentence will possess marked poetical beauty. His ability in this respect is due in part to natural literary aptitude and in part to early and painstaking practice. He tells us at the beginning of his ministerial life—I quote his own words : ' I sought to interest men by natural conceptions, polished sentences, and vivid and striking metaphors : I found it did not keep them.' But the power of clear and beautiful expression is no longer his main reliance ; it is rather like the polish and ornamental scroll-work on the flashing blade of the rapier.

"I trust that I have not minimised Mr. Meyer's natural gifts for the sake of proving a point. I am very confident, however, that his great power does not emanate from brawn or brain, or from social, linguistic, or oratorical graces, singly or in combination, but that it emerges out

of the depths of a life hidden in God. Whatever gift or grace
was his—of writing, speaking, working, suffering—he
deliberately laid upon the altar eighteen years ago, and the
fire of the Holy Ghost descended upon the sacrifice."

The Canadian impression given by Canon E. C. Earp,
of Saskatoon, fresh from contact with the preacher in his
real vocation, completes the portrait.

" To see him enter the pulpit one might imagine that the
weight of nearly fourscore years was a burden too great to
be borne. But as he begins to speak the years seem to fall
away from him. His clear voice rings out to the farthest
corners of a great church. His cultured accents fall on the
ear like sweet music. His modulated tones articulate each
word to its full value and on his face there shines the light
which comes from close communion with God.

" His method of preaching is a rebuke to those reformers
who add to the general confusion by their reckless energy.
His measured sentences proceed from thought to thought,
carrying his hearers with him along a mental pathway from
which none can err. He brings tolerance and calm as he
declares the everlasting purposes of the Eternal God.
Around him is an indescribable air of gentleness and
goodness. He adorns the ministerial office and is numbered
among the great preachers who interpret the way of God to
man. There is no striving after effect, the grand simplicity
of his message makes its own appeal. His sincerity is as
clear as the light and is an unconscious revelation of the
soul within.

" The result of his preaching in Saskatoon has been to
bring many of us back to where we ought to be. He has
recalled us from our waywardness to that higher realm of
life wherein the soul delights to do the will of God. He has
emphasised the vital and fundamental Christian verities
which unite the various communions in the fellowship of
the Catholic Church of Christ.

" It is impossible to calculate the good derived from such
a faithful servant of God. After seeing large crowds and

receiving generous offerings, we must remember that the higher statistics are in the hands of God.

" We humbly pray a blessing upon this chosen servant of the Lord and upon the work that remains for him to do. May years of happy service be his before he is called upon to take the journey home ! With a life fulfilled and with a task accomplished the journey will be but brief, for earth seems now to blend with heaven in the soul of F. B. Meyer."

CHAPTER TWENTY

A Bundle of Incidents

THESE incidents are gathered together without any sequence. They all illuminate Dr. Meyer's characteristics and methods, his readiness to witness for the Master and to give a helping hand to other people.

One afternoon in a tram-car in North London, he noticed on the opposite seat an elderly woman with a basket, evidently a charwoman returning from her day's work. She appeared to be anything but happy, and as the car emptied only he and she were left. Then, having recognised him all along, she summoned up courage to speak to him and, calling him by name, she told him her story. As a widow she had been left alone in the world except for her crippled daughter who, in spite of her affliction, was a continual joy to her. Every evening, as she explained, when she came home from her work she knew her daughter was in the room where they lived, ready to greet her. She was always there, and at night in the darkness she could stretch out her hand and know she was there, too. She made tea in the morning, and left her for the day, but she knew all the time that her daughter was there to greet her with a glad face when she returned. " And now," she said sadly, " now she is dead, and I am alone, and I am miserable : I am going home, and it is scarcely home, for she is not there."

There was little time for discussion, but Meyer was "At attention !" for his Master on the moment. " When you get home and put the key in the door," he said, " say aloud, ' Jesus, I know You are here,' and be ready to greet Him directly you open the door. And as you light the fire tell Him what has happened during the day ; if anybody has been kind, tell Him, if anybody has been unkind, tell Him, just as you would have told your daughter. Be sure, to make your cup of tea. At night stretch out your hand in the darkness and say, ' Jesus, I know You are here.' " Then the tram-car reached the terminus, and they parted.

Some months afterwards he happened to be in the same neighbourhood again and, singularly enough, the woman who sat in the opposite seat of the car greeted him by name. " You don't know me, Mr. Meyer," she said. " I am afraid I do not," he replied. Then she reminded him of the interview some months before. " But you are not the same woman," he said in astonishment. " Oh, yes, I am," she said. " I did as you told me. I went home and said, ' Jesus, I know You are here,' and I kept on saying it, and it has made all the difference in my life, and now I feel I know Him." And the change in her face bore witness to the truth of her story.

A young girl on first coming to London had to make a journey south of the Thames in a busy part, at the peak hour of the workers' scramble. She managed to get a footing in a crowded tram-car, and was feeling very tired and rather frightened when a voice said " I think I can make room for you here." Looking down she saw a gentleman wearing an Inverness cloak. He pulled it aside and drew her down, half carrying her, at his side, at the same time saying, " I am so sorry not to be able to give you my seat, but last evening, when I did so for a young girl, I had to leave the car as it was overcrowded, and was late for my meeting. I have a meeting to-night so dare not risk it again." So writes Miss Mary Swift.

One of his oldest members, when suffering from a great depression of spirit because of a serious disappointment in her life, met him in middle aisle of the church. At once he detected the sorrowful look and knowing something of the

circumstances he said to her, " I know just what you are
going through." " Ah, Dr. Meyer," she responded, " I am
in a perfect Slough of Despond." " Yes," he quickly replied,
" but there are stepping-stones there." The next morning
she received a letter from him with words of comfort : he
must have gone straight into his vestry and have written
it, and months afterwards, when she met him again, she was
able with a glad heart to say, " I have found the stepping-
stones."

A lady, who on occasion typed some of Dr. Meyer's
manuscripts, unfortunately lost two articles of his among
her papers. Of course, she wrote him very penitently, and
she treasures his reply. Instead of chiding her he says :—

" Thank you for yours. I can imagine your distress. Think
no more of it and we will halve the loss. I think it was a good
thing, as my second attempt was an improvement.
                                        " Yours,
                                            " F. B. M."

At another time when Dr. Meyer returned the account
for some work which the same journalist had taken to his
house as it was wanted quickly, he added in his own handwriting, " To shoe leather, a shilling."

Years ago Dr. Meyer promised to preach at Chiswick
Baptist Chapel on a certain Thursday. By some inadvert-
ence he was advertised for the Thursday following, instead
of the correct day. As a result he came to the church and
found the door shut. The Rev. A. E. Edgerton, discovering
the mistake too late to prevent him coming, wrote a letter
of regret. But before Dr. Meyer could have received it, he
sent a gracious note, saying he had been to the church door,
and was sorry he could not come the next week. Then in
reply to the letter of apology he wrote, again without a word
of vexation, " Do not trouble, nothing happens by chance,
and the rather long walk, in the calm autumn air, did me
good."

It is a mistake to imagine that Dr. Meyer was sanctimonious. He was entirely natural. On one occasion in the Midlands he was entertained to lunch before an afternoon meeting, and one of the guests, mistaking the situation, almost absorbed the conversation with unctuous platitudes, which he evidently imagined befitted the occasion. When they rose from the table Dr. Meyer went to the window and suddenly turning to the astonished company said, " I wonder who has won the Derby ? " It happened to be Derby Day. It is a question whether he enjoyed more the shocked expression of the well-meaning talker or the laughter of the rest of the company, so skilfully set at their ease.

A girl employed as a folder in a book-binding establishment was interested in one of Dr. Meyer's little books, and read part of the pages as she folded them. She was so captivated that she hid some of the leaves in her frock and read them at night, Dr. Carlile tells us. As she read, her interest deepened, and before the morning she had given her allegiance to her Saviour. She took the leaves back and, as soon as she had the money, purchased a copy of the little book. She was afterwards baptized at the church at John Street, Bedford Row.

The Rev. Arthur S. Langley, in an interesting letter, says : " General William Booth and Dr. Meyer were addressing a crowded meeting of missionaries and deaconesses in the Central Hall, Manchester, at the invitation of the City Mission. He saw that there was just one little boy present—he was blowing the organ. After the meeting he sought out that boy—who is the writer—and the General and the Doctor laid their hands on him and blessed him."

Very cordial relationship existed between the ministers of Christ Church and the Metropolitan Tabernacle. In June, 1927, Rev. H. Tydeman Chilvers invited Dr. Meyer to conduct both services on a Sunday in the Tabernacle, not only for the services themselves, which were very largely attended, but as a sign of the happy fellowship existing between the ministers of these two large centres of Christian witness and activity.

In the previous year when, on different errands, they were both in America, their paths crossed at the Conference at Stonybrook in the State of New York. When Mr. Chilvers arrived, the darkness had fallen, the Conference Hall was, of course, closed, and he would have been altogether desolate had not Dr. Meyer, in his thoughtfulness, been at the door to receive him. "Welcome, dear boy," he said, and, guessing how a stranger would feel in a strange land, he clasped him in his arms as a father might have gripped his son. It was too late for a meal, though the traveller was hungry, but Meyer managed to forage some tea and toast, which they enjoyed together in his little room, both sitting on the bed. Then said Meyer, "You are too tired to pray. I will pray to-night," and after prayer he conducted Chilvers to his room. Each night afterwards they had tea and toast and prayer, both joining in the meagre feast, each alternately taking the prayer. And with walks in the woods they cemented their friendship, the younger man much encouraged, the elder, though he did not parade it, like Paul in the olden time, greatly cheered by the coming of Titus.

By some misadventure Dr. Meyer had promised to be at two meetings at the same time—one of them at the Tabernacle. He wrote to Mr. Chilvers affirming his willingness to come, adding :—

"But if you could get through without me, I would gladly fulfil the other engagement, which was prior. If only we were in Heaven and had wings, I could do both !

"Yours affect.,

"F. B. MEYER."

Dr. Cuyler boasted that there was one thing that should be reckoned to him for righteousness—he had never compiled a hymn book. But Dr. Meyer could not make that boast, for in collaboration with Rev. W. J. Mayers he compiled "Hymns for Heart and Life," for use in meetings which in early days they frequently conducted together. Mr. Mayers tells with some glee that when at the Memorial Service for D. L. Moody, Meyer gave an address and he sang a solo, the rumour got abroad that it was Meyer that had sung.

It was one of his pleasantries when people complained to him that he was doing too much—" Oh, you are mistaken, there are three of us and you are mixing us up." The three were F. B. Meyer, W. J. Mayers, and J. B. Myers, the last one of the Secretaries of the Baptist Missionary Society. Mr. Mayers says that in Australia, when he was there on behalf of Dr. Barnardo's Homes, people frequently thanked him for his writings in *The Christian*.

The Rev. George W. McPherson writes : " Dr. Meyer could easily have become a man of some wealth, but in this respect he mastered himself perfectly. He was very frank over money matters. He told his representative in America just what honorarium he would expect to receive, and it was very modest, considering his heavy travelling expenses. When he was in his final service at Tent Evangel, concluding eight sermons in a series, I said to the audience : ' We shall now give a love-offering to our dear driend whose face we may see no more.' While the offering was being taken, I glanced at Dr. Meyer and his face was buried deeply in his hands and it was evident that he was pained over what we were doing. After the Finance Committee had counted the offering I went at once to the hotel and handed Dr. Meyer a cheque for the full amount received. It was much larger than the sum he had understood he was to receive, in fact it was the largest offering ever taken in Tent Evangel. But he refused to accept it, saying, ' You will give me my usual stipend, the remainder you will keep to help defray the heavy expenses of the mission. If I were to take this money for preaching Christ, it would get abroad that Meyer is growing rich from his missionary work. Gossip would carry it to England, and it would be growing larger as it travels.' "

In a certain town Dr. Meyer visited with some frequency, he was waited on by his host's chauffeur, who helped to carry him upstairs, prepared his bath and otherwise helped him. Ted was making a doll's house for his children, and Dr. Meyer insisted on furnishing one of the rooms, and did it.

" Dr. F. B. Meyer presents his respects to the young house-keepers, who are about to live in this new home, and begs them to accept this suite of furniture for the dining room. May they have a long and happy experience of this gift made through his friend ' Ted.'

" F. B. MEYER."

On the fly-leaf of the Bible used by Rev. T. Wilkinson Riddle, Mr. Meyer wrote in January, 1909 : " Never be startled at the temptations that assail, or the trouble through which your life travels. They are the predestined teachers of those deeper lessons for which men are waiting and which you can only learn by suffering and conquering." Mr. Riddle tells that when he was about seventeen years of age, and had begun to preach, having devoured a number of the cheap reprints of standard works, he rattled off their names to Mr. Meyer, who, with gentle satire, replied that there were thousands of books he had never even heard the titles of, and brushed aside all he had done as only desultory reading. Then he gave him practical advice which proved of the utmost value in his career.

The Guardian of May 5th, 1927, says : " Dr. Meyer was not himself a pacifist, but he was a staunch upholder of the rights of conscience, and he greatly interested himself in the C.O. movement. He is one of the very few outsiders who has been allowed, in the course of its 260 years' history, to address the Meeting for Sufferers of the Society of Friends, its executive committee, as he did on one occasion in 1916. He was evidently a little taken aback that at the close of his plea for C.O's there was, according to Quaker custom, no applause. He, with some other Free Church ministers, went to see Lord Kitchener only a few days before the latter went on his fatal journey, on behalf of the objectors and received his permission to visit those who, contrary to Mr. Asquith's pledge, had been hurried over to France.

After a visit to the men who had consented to work in the non-combatant corps some miles towards the line at the back of Boulogne, Dr. Meyer was taken to see the thirty-four men, including several Quakers, in the Military Punishment Barracks at Boulogne, from which a few days later they were led out to receive the death sentence, afterwards commuted to ten years' penal servitude. In the presence of Colonel Wilberforce, the port commandant, he addressed each of the men, and there seems little doubt that the evidence that the military authorities thus received that their willingness to make an ' example ' of these C.O's was being closely watched by many in England, really saved their lives and the reputation of this country.

" Dr. Meyer's untiring efforts on behalf of these men, for he also paid several visits to individuals in guard rooms and at Pentonville prison, were all the more noteworthy because he had himself lost his only grandson but a few months before."

Dr. Meyer himself recounts the following : " Some years ago I came on the remarkable text, Galatians iii. 14. It appeared to me as though no one had ever discovered it before. At least, I wondered that it seemed to no one what it seemed to me, for I had been so long and deeply exercised as to the conditions of receiving the Holy Spirit. Now this verse leapt out of the page and accosted me : ' That we might receive the promise of the Spirit through faith.' ' Through faith ! ' I said to myself, ' Through faith ! ' But that is precisely the way in which we receive salvation ; and if that be all, it is possible to claim my share in the fulness of the Holy Spirit, as I claimed my share in the salvation wrought out by Jesus on the Cross.' It seemed as though a voice spoke in my soul—' As you claimed forgiveness from the hands of the dying Christ, so claim the fulness of blessing from those of the living Christ.' With all humility and obedience I took that position and preferred my claim, and turning to the whole passage, of which these words are a part, it seemed as though grace were given to appropriate the full terms of the promise made to Abraham, that God would bless, and make a blessing, and that all the ends of the earth might be blessed through the influence of one frail life."

And he also instances another text of Scripture: " Almost the greatest revelation that ever came to me was through the words, ' We shall be saved by His life ' (Rom. v. 10), coupled with the words in verse 17—' They that *receive* the abundance of grace shall reign in life through the One.' I saw that the differences which obtained among the children of God were due to their ability or inability to receive the incoming tides of the life of the Son of God. For months my life seemed to alternate between these two poles of thought. Now, I said to myself, I am reconciled ; but I need more than reconciliation—I require saving—and this shall be mine ; not by looking back on an event which transpired so many years ago, not by holding a creed, not by accepting a system of doctrine, but by opening every avenue of my being *to His life*, I shall be saved ' by His life.' Then I would turn to the other verse, and realise that there was an abundance of grace and gift for all, but that only those who received it could reign, could exert a regal authority on others, in this life and the next."

Dr. Wilbur Chapman, breakfasting at Mr. Moody's house where Dr. Meyer was a guest, asked him if he could explain why his experience seemed so intermittent ; sometimes he felt full of power in his ministry, sometimes his heart was empty. Apparently changing the subject, Dr. Meyer asked him if he had ever tried to breathe out three times, without breathing in once ? Quite off his guard, Dr. Chapman tried the experiment, and of course failed, upon which, Meyer simply said, " Don't you know you must always breathe in before you breathe out, and the one must be in proportion to the other ? " That solved the problem.

CHAPTER TWENTY-ONE

The Keswick Outlook

PROBABLY the most beautiful vista in the world is from the terrace of St. John's Church at Keswick, looking down Derwentwater. Mr. W. T. Stead years ago asked the readers of the *Review of Reviews* to vote as to the loveliest view in Great Britain, and this was the scene chosen by a great majority. At the moment the beauty is a little less beautiful because of a tree that has grown too high in the Rector's garden, but that can easily be remedied.

The Convention which Canon Battersby established could have no more wonderful setting. If Strength and Beauty are in the Sanctuary of God then both are here. Skiddaw and Scawfell in massive grandeur vie with the charm of the lake and Friar's Crag ; and the Tent with its three pennons flying, Love, Joy, Peace, is not the Tabernacle in the Wilderness, but the Pavilion of God where elect souls have often had days of heaven on earth.

It is impossible to think of Dr. Meyer without thinking of Keswick, of which he was, in large measure, the embodiment : and equally impossible to think of Keswick, even to-day, without thinking of Dr. Meyer, one of its oldest and most trusted speakers, and for many years a member of its Council. A freshly descriptive narrative of his early appearance on the Keswick platform and his subsequent ministry of the teaching associated with Keswick, was written by Prebendary Webster, himself one of the most welcome of Keswick speakers.

" For many years Mr. Meyer attended more Conventions for the deepening of spiritual life than any other speaker. It mattered not in what part of the United Kingdom or

Ireland the meetings were to be held, Mr. Meyer was one of the first to be invited by the local committee, for no one was more acceptable to Churchmen and Nonconformists alike, and the evening he spoke (so many enquiries were made that the secret was not often kept) would generally be the fullest evening in the week. It was not because he was the deepest teacher in the Keswick Brotherhood or that he surpassed all others in exegetical skill ; the movement has still its theologians and at that time had its poet even more gifted in fulness of exposition and soul-uplifting clearness of vision than Mr. Meyer. It was Mr. Meyer's personality even more than his message which made him such an honoured favourite.

" Not that he lacked the distinct message which we associate with Keswick. I well remember my first feeling when I heard that Mr. Meyer was going to speak at Keswick. At that time, in the eighties, Mr. Meyer was very prominent as a speaker at Blue-Ribbon meetings, and the writer had some apprehension as to whether this Temperance orator had really experienced the definite and distinct blessing which was looked upon as the indispensable qualification for a speaker at the Keswick Convention. His fears were immediately dispelled. It was plain to all that Mr. Meyer (partly owing to the influence of the Cambridge seven) had received a real lift in his spiritual life and was bringing all his great powers of preaching and persuasion to the task of helping others to get the same lift.

" One of his early addresses at Keswick was on the incident of our Lord walking on the water. He drew the contrast between the slow and laborious progress of the disciples as they toiled at the oar and the swift, dignified, easy progress of the Master as He walked on the sea. He dwelt upon the ambition awakened in Peter to imitate the Master's triumphant walk, justifying our instinctive longing for a life of rest and victory by the text, ' As He is so are we in this world.' And with real spiritual power, as well as most winsome poetic beauty, he made every one dissatisfied with the old life of striving and self-effort, and constrained us by his personal magnetism to abandon ourselves without reserve to a life of absolute and fearless reliance upon Christ.

" And what a magnetic personality he was, This is what I mean in saying that it was the man more than the message that was so attractive. Comparatively few of the many scores of addresses I have heard from Mr. Meyer stand out now in my memory, but the conviction abides that no one was more helpful at a Convention and no personality more spiritually effective.

" This, perhaps, was felt quite as much out of the meetings as in them. How he shone at the social meal. The conversation never flagged or wandered about amongst frivolities. Some absorbing interest—some matter touching the kingdom—some new phase of truth—some helpful book—some practical difficulty on which light was needed was sure to be suggested by his fertile brain and the whole company enriched by his intelligent and sympathetic handling of it. And yet it was, of course, in the meeting and the after-meeting that he excelled.

" As a speaker he was second to none. His articulation was perfect, and though not gifted with a voice of extra-ordinary power, his speaking was pleasant and sympathetic and not a word was dropped. He was not a passioned orator and was rarely carried away by his feelings ; but when speaking in the power of the Spirit the very quietness of his style was deeply impressive. His chief gift was his sympathy, his power of getting into touch with his audience, and carrying them along with him. He could speak out unpleasant truths boldly and fearlessly, but he never gave offence.

" I am not sure that Mr. Meyer was as good at Keswick (I have noticed the same of other speakers) as at the provincial Conventions. Dozens of times I have been with him on the platform in Birmingham, Nottingham, Bridge of Allan and other centres and marvelled and praised God for his mastery over the meeting and his peculiar power to adapt himself to his audience and lift his hearers into the almost seen Presence of God. But at Keswick, too,

Mr. Meyer has been blessed to hundreds, and quite as much in his personal heart-to-heart talks and conversations round the supper table as in his set addresses."

The Keswick Convention stands for one thing and yet at intervals efforts have been made to make it stand for something else. Its testimony is that the Living Christ, received by faith as the Saviour, can also by faith give instant and constant deliverance from sin, the Holy Spirit making the truth, apprehended by faith, effective in experience and conduct—that and nothing beside.

Naturally there follows such an experience a mode of living. It may be puritanic, mystical, aggressive, but that is the fruit of experience, different in different cases—but it is not the experience. Where there is the initial renunciation of all known sin and utter abandonment to Christ, the rest follows.

But at different times different people have sought to add to this theme, or to lead the movement at a tangent. I am not sure that Dr. Meyer himself, in his militant days, did not almost make the attempt. But to turn the purely spiritual on to legal, social, theological, or hysterical lines, is to frustrate the very end it has in view.

Had Dr. Meyer as a Baptist declared it impossible to receive those who accept a formula which implies baptismal regeneration, he would have been as far from the unity in Christ as some who endeavour to impose other tests, and yet he might have had more justification. But at the beginning and at the end he rejoiced that we are " all one in Christ Jesus."

As an instance of the care taken to safeguard the sacred deposit of truth committed to the Convention, and the confidence placed in Mr. Meyer, the following letter from the Rev. Evan Hopkins, placed at our disposal by the courtesy of Principal Evans of Spurgeon's College, may be quoted :—

" *5th April*, 1890.

" MY DEAR MEYER,

" I wrote to Canon Westcott about his note in his Commentary on 1 John i. 7, and this morning I received his reply.

His letter is too long for me now to give you a copy, but of course he disclaimed all thoughts of sinlessness. He says, ' The ambiguity as to my meaning in the note to which you refer had not occurred to me,' and after saying what he does mean by his note he adds most humbly as it seems to me, ' If I have an opportunity I will endeavour to guard against the misapprehension of my words. Just now I cannot give sufficient thought to the subject.'

" He takes the words 1 John i. 7, as describing the ultimate effect of the blood. He does say ' *when* the glorious end is reached, for of this the Apostle says nothing. It is enough for us to know what is God's purpose for us, and that the sacrifice of Christ is sufficient for its attainment . . .' Do you feel inclined to send me something short for May number of *L. of F.* ? It would be very acceptable.

" Ever yours affecty.,
" EVAN H. HOPKINS."

Not only in public ministry but in many a quiet talk Dr. Meyer brought blessing to troubled souls and established others in the faith. Mr. Frederick Wood traces the beginning of the Young Life Movement to an interview with him at Keswick, and speaks of an hour of prayer in Dr. Meyer's room as the time of his ordination.

It was a delightful circumstance that Dr. Inwood and Dr. Meyer were called on in the 1928 Convention to speak together on an evening when two other speakers had fallen out of the programme, and those who were present at the meeting when these two veterans each spoke for the last time, recall with awe the power that rested on their message.

Then when Dr. Meyer presided over the first Communion Service held in the Tent, some three thousand Christians from all the churches and from many parts of the world sharing with joyance in the solemn feast, it was not only the climax to the Convention itself, but a crown to all the years of the past for the man who had so often fed Christ's people there on the finest of the wheat

CHAPTER TWENTY-TWO

On Pilgrimage

It is impossible to give any adequate account of the journeys undertaken by Dr. Meyer in pursuance of the Mission with which he was entrusted. As in Wesley's case, and to a much fuller degree, the world was his parish. During these years of pilgrimage he visited Europe, Jamaica, the United States, Canada, the Near East, India, China, South Africa and Australia. He had so many crossings of the Atlantic Ocean that he lost count of them. To a meeting on one occasion Dr. Clifford introduced him as " Dr. Meyer, the ubiquitous."

I. Europe.

In the memorial resolution passed by the Evangelical Alliance on May 23rd, 1929, it is recalled that he was " a frequent and much beloved delegate and speaker at the Blankenburg (Germany) Evangelical Alliance Conference." On the eightieth birthday of the Alliance he wrote, " I was first brought into living touch with the Alliance in 1869–70, and have always observed the first week in the New Year." Alone, or with Rev. W. Fuller Gooch, he was often welcomed to the great gathering of Evangelical people gathered from all corners of Germany.

" Blankenburg," wrote Dr. Meyer, " is a lovely village, situate among the pine-covered hills of Thurangia. The Conference owed much of its early interest to the presence and interest of Fraulein von Weling, at whose invitation I went to represent our British movement. Those who crowd the beautiful new hall on the slope of the hill can hardly imagine the simplicity of the early beginning, when the meetings were held in the school-house, just beneath the level of the terrace. The dear lady herself was my interpreter and it was a perfect luxury to address the eager German folk through her lips. Indeed, with her beside me, translation rather added to the force of the message. These addresses were subsequently published and widely circulated, carrying in many directions the message of salvation."

On three occasions Dr. Meyer was present at this Convention, and here he formed an intimate friendship with Pastor Stockmayer who, he says, " of all men that I have met most perfectly exemplified the strength and nobility of life hidden with Christ in God."

Growing out of Blankenburg, two Conferences were arranged in Berlin by Count Bernstorff, after which there were tours through other parts of Germany, with him. In 1907, the Rev. Julius Rohrbach, now of Wilmette, Illinois, was his translator, and he speaks of many of the German nobility, ministers of the Gospel, and Christian workers sharing in the spiritual blessings of the visit.

A prolonged tour of Northern Europe was made in 1902. After a hurriedly arranged meeting at Hamburg, Dr. Meyer passed over to Norway, and from Christiana, where he had some services, he crossed to Sweden, spending three days each in Jonköping and Orebo on his way to Stockholm.

But his chief objective was Södertalge, a watering place about an hour's journey south of the city, where a notable Conference is convened year by year, having a similar place in Sweden as the Keswick Convention has in this country. It owes its inception and success largely to the influence of Prince and Princess Bernadotte, the Prince presiding at all the meetings and mingling freely with the guests.

Back to Stockholm where, in passing, he had had a Bible Reading in the home of the Prince and Princess, which was attended by the Queen of Sweden ; he enjoyed a Sunday crowded with services, which were attended by throngs. Next to Spurgeon the writings of Meyer are the most popular devotional reading in Sweden.

Then on to Helsingfors, in Finland, for some days, and to St. Petersburg for a brief visit, seeing in each city gracious signs of God's presence. Afterwards, at the invitation of Count Joachim Von Molte, he journeyed to Copenhagen, where the buildings were not capable of holding the crowds.

II. JAMAICA.

In November of the same year, 1902, Dr. Meyer visited Jamiaca, and left again on Christmas Day for the return journey. Here the enthusiastic scenes that he had witnessed in other places were outdone. Cordial welcome was given to him by all sections of the Church of Christ, and people thronged to his meetings.

III. THE UNITED STATES.

Chapter Three contains a personal narrative of some of Dr. Meyer's experiences in the United States characteristic of others, but when he visited the Southern States on his tenth visit to America he had some experiences worthy of special record. His mission began in South Carolina, then passed on to New Orleans, across Texas and on to Los Angeles, afterwards to Portland, Oregon, and then back to New York. Los Angeles seems to have risen to greet him. " He is not the masterful platform orator that one listens to while sitting under the preaching of Campbell Morgan, but as a mystic and as one who blends the metaphysical with the spiritual and makes known the power of God which may manifest itself through the faculties and emotions of the human mind, he has no peer on either continent. His keen apprehension and comprehension of the words of Scripture in their application to human need and thought comes forth at times like a Divine inspiration, and his most conservative auditor is ready to exclaim ' Surely this man is none the less than an oracle of God.' "

His simplicity seems to have impressed those pioneers of the Pacific. " I just want people to be natural," said their visitor. " I can't bear a man looking good—or trying to. I hate anything like pretence." Quite openly they called him a tenderfoot, but he took it all in good part, and met unconventional people on their own terms, greatly to the success of his work.

A Sunday was spent at San Diego, and then after another day at Los Angeles Mr. Meyer went on to Portland. *The Pacific Baptist*, published in that city, in its issue for May 3rd, 1905, says :—

" Mr. Meyer's first series of addresses in this country—given, we believe, about eight years ago—were later published in a small volume entitled, from the subject of the first address, ' A Castaway.' On the Pacific Coast he has in the main followed the themes presented in this book. No better general view of his teaching, therefore, can be given than to indicate the subjects of these earlier addresses. He begins with an appeal for performance of God's will lest God should cease to use a man and he become a castaway. Coupled with this is the proclamation of the gospel that though the life has once been grievously marred through sin, God can make that life over. Then follow five addresses both illustrative of the truth that two natures struggle within each soul and indicative of the way of victory for the Christian. These are discussions of ' the natural and the spiritual man,' ' the substitution of the Christ-life for the self-life,' ' Christ the complement of our need,' ' deliverance from the power of sin,' and ' God's two men.' The eighth and ninth addresses are devoted to two aspects of Pentecost as the ' anointing ' and the ' infilling ' of the Holy Spirit, while the last chapter of the book is a deeply mystical and highly practical talk upon ' heart-rest.'

" Mr. Meyer is ever speaking of the things of the Spirit. With rare simplicity he illustrates, repeats, amplifies his position until almost any utterance of his may be expected to show unseen realities to eyes blinded with sense, and to lead hearts choked with the cares of this world to pray for the gift of the Holy Ghost. Because the expressions in the chapter on ' The Anointing with the Holy Spirit ' are the most definite, and because the theme is central with the preacher, let us take from that chapter what Mr. Meyer terms the five conditions of receiving the Holy Spirit. First, you cannot have the power of the Holy Ghost without having the Holy Ghost Himself—which is as much as to say that if the Spirit is desired primarily for what He can give of power, you wish it and not Him. Secondly, you must be cleansed : God cannot tolerate an unclean dwelling for His Spirit. Thirdly, you must live for the glory of Christ as your supreme end : the Spirit is not given till Jesus is glorified. Fourthly, your teaching must be in harmony with the Word of God : all this emphasis upon the Spirit is not a mystic's contempt of the objective revelation in the Bible : ' let the Holy Ghost fill you, but He will work along that Book.' Fifthly, the Holy Spirit must be received by faith : Galatians iii. 14, is the battle-axe—' That we might receive the promise of the Spirit through faith,' for the reception of God's gifts is not conditioned upon the testimony of the senses."

IV. CANADA.

In the later years of his life Dr. Meyer gave Canada a large proportion of the time he spent on the American continent. He was a familiar figure in Toronto. At one time he attended the Ontario Convention of Baptist Churches there, giving addresses daily, at another he conducted a series of meetings in John Knox Presbyterian Church. And in most of the cities of Ontario, such as Hamilton, Preston and London, he is gratefully remembered, as also in the cities of other provinces, Montreal, Winnipeg, Saskatoon, Edmonton.

He speaks at one time of a morning meeting of sixty-five ministers, at another of forty-two ministers : of people coming in from a thirty-mile radius to be present at the large gatherings of the afternoon and evening. Typical of other cities, extracts may be given from the *Calgary Albertan* :—

" Dr. Meyer sat on the edge of a table and talked to the ministers in a free and easy style. He first told them how much he had enjoyed visiting Canada, and after referring to its great future, congratulated those present upon having the opportunity of moulding the thoughts and lives of the people.

" He said his whole life had been influenced by a criticism of Mr. Birrell, of Liverpool, after he had preached a topical sermon, who said : ' Meyer, that was quite a good sermon you preached but it was on a topic. There will come a time when you will have spoken on all the topics and the newspapers will have excelled you. Where will you be then ? You had better learn to expound the Word of God.'

" ' And,' said Dr. Meyer, ' I have done that ever since, and any success I may have had in preaching or in writing my books was due to that advice, and because I have endeavoured to open up the unsearchable riches of God.' "

Describing his journey in the far West, he says in a letter to his Church at home :—" It is difficult to describe that tour, because everything is so novel to English eyes. The long, level, single line of rails, the miles on miles of apparently waste land—then the knowledge of cornfields stretching three hundred miles north, many of the farmsteads standing alone, the large areas marked out for the new young cities, only a small part being reclaimed, the simplicity of the home-life, where no domestic servants are required. It is all so wonderful and interesting : and everywhere I met people who had read my books, or had heard me preach in the homeland, and so many people keep turning up who have been more or less connected with Christ Church."

V. The Near East.

" In 1909," Dr. Meyer wrote, " two meetings gave me their God-speed as I started for a tour in Eastern Europe. One at the Chapter House, St. Paul's, where the Archdeacon of London invited a number of leading Churchmen and Nonconformists to meet me, and the other at Aldersgate Street Y.M.C.A. The bells were ringing for evening prayer in St. Paul's Cathedral during our meeting, and I did realise the sense in which one belongs to everything English. I went forth to be a blessing to the One Church."

After a journey across snow-clad Europe he reached Philoppopolis, where his chief interest lay in six meetings with fifteen Bulgarian pastors. He had crowded meetings in the noble stone church holding about five hundred people. From thence he passed on to Constantinople, where he spent ten days addressing Turks, Greeks, Jews, Armenians and Europeans. On two occasions he had the opportunity of speaking to congregations of Spanish Jews at their Saturday gatherings. The Dutch Church was crowded day after day for his meetings ; and three times he addressed about four hundred students at Robert College on the straits, and at the close, at the request of the students the professors withdrew, leaving him alone amongst this crowd of young fellows. He says " it was an exciting and memorable hour."

Smyrna was next visited and the site of ancient Ephesus. " On Easter Eve, at midnight, we looked down on a crowd of five thousand people, assembled in the darkness beneath us and waiting with unlit torches for the handing out from behind the altar of the Church of the newly-kindled Easter flame. As the hour of midnight approached the expectancy became most intense, till suddenly a lighted torch was reached out, from which the flame passed rapidly from rank to rank, and in a very short while all the torches were glowing and night was as bright as day. I have often thought of this as an apt illustration of the spread of God's Love from heart to heart. But, alas ! how many torches that might be lit are still dark ! "

From Smyrna Dr. Meyer found his way to Alexandria, calling at Athens. But eight years previously he had visited Beyrout for a Conference at Brummana, held there in a tent erected in the grounds of the Boys' Training Home.

A considerable number of letters have been preserved testifying to the blessing received by the missionaries who gathered from Syria, Palestine and Egypt. It will suffice to give one written by a man whose name is honoured in all missionary circles :—

" Lebanon Hotel, Brummâna, Syria.

" Sunday evening, 19/8/1901.

" MY DEAR MR. MEYER,

" My wife and I both wish to give you and your wife a warm farewell, even though we have not said so in person. May God bring you both safely home again, none the worse physically, and rejoicing in the Lord. It seemed to me to-night as if these Bible-lands had drawn very near to one another, and that the Lord was cementing the friendships made while here into a holy bond of prayer and fellowship that will never be broken. We were one body as we all partook this afternoon of one Bread. Long may we remain so, but with ever-increasing growth and power and usefulness !

" I do not want to ask you to make any promise of prayer that will be a burden to you. But *whenever you remember Beyrout and Damascus in prayer, will you call to mind as well that Cairo is twice as big as both put together.* Remember the 99.5% of the women of Egypt who are illiterate, and degraded beyond comparison with these Syrian girls. Remember the 700 Moslem teachers in Cairo, of the 13,000 Moslem pupils between 12 and 30 years old, and the 13,000 boys from 7 to 11, round about.

" While you think of the 50,000 Jews in Jerusalem, remember also the 20,000 more Jews in Cairo and Alexandria almost uncared for. And when you remember the 500 Syrian Beyrout College men, remember also the 1,500 foreign students in Cairo, from India and Morocco and Hausaland to Afghanistan. But more than all the little band of a dozen or more enquirers, most of them students, others from various tribes, and some more not followed up in the villages.

" Now good-bye—you will have enough of other notes to read. *Bon voyage.* Adieu.

" Yours gratefully and rememberingly, in our Victorious Lord,

" DOUGLAS M. THORNTON."

VI. CHINA.

From the Near East Mr. Meyer, in 1909, went to the Far East, representing the Keswick Convention. Early in his journey he wrote : " Too late in life I learn what I have missed in not being a missionary." First of all he visited Malaya, holding meetings in Penang and Taeping and Singapore. Then he spent some time in Hong Kong, and was able to be in Canton for four days. It was a surprise to find himself in these places denounced by some earnest brethren as a heretic, but this irony did not hinder the success of his visits.

At Amoy he discovered the catechist of W. C. Burns, the saintly missionary to China, and from his lips heard some of the deeply interesting reminiscences of that consecrated life. Foochow, and the hill station at Kuliang, were next visited, and then via Shanghai, the four summer resorts of Moh Kanshan, Kuling, Cheefoo and Peitaiho.

" There can be no question to those who have heard Mr. Meyer in years gone by and are privileged to hear him again," writes the Rev. Nelson Bitton, at that time missionary in Shanghai, " that he has gained tremendously in power by a remarkable gift of sympathetic tenderness. Cannot the Free Churches," he adds, " see to it that Mr. Meyer is made a new Apostle to the Gentiles ? " At the foot of the sheet containing Mr. Bitton's article there is an interesting note—" From all I hear I fully endorse every word that Mr. Bitton says and more. Timothy Richard." Ten years afterwards, Mr. D. E. Hoste of the China Inland Mission writes, " I shall never forget your stay with us at Shanghai and the influence of your life and ministry among us."

With some satisfaction Mr. Meyer notes that by the good hand of God upon him in this journey he travelled no less than 25,000 miles and that, in spite of the intense heat, he had not broken one appointment. Returning by the Siberian Railway he entered upon his second pastorate at Regent's Park Chapel.

VII. India

Ten years before this visit to China Mr. Meyer landed at Bombay on Christmas Eve, 1898. In various journals and magazines he describes his Mediterranean voyage and his first experience of the Indian Ocean, which, if the limits of this book allowed, would be interesting to reproduce. At Bombay services were held, and also at Lahore, Agra and Cawnpore. Ludhiana was visited, Lucknow, Benares, and Allahabad, and of course Calcutta. But nothing can profitably be written about these cities that cannot be found in missionary books, though all are described in Mr. Meyer's glowing language. Should there be a call for a reprint of these vivid travel-talks perhaps the publishers may be able to respond to it.

In Madras distinct blessing was recorded : in Rangoon memories of Judson crowded upon him : and at Madura, at Palamacottah and at Colombo in Ceylon successful meetings were held.

In his little book, *The Wideness of God's Mercy*, he emphasises one result of his Indian experiences. " At the close of an afternoon service in one of the public halls of Bombay, a number of intelligent and thoughtful men gathered round me, who said that my teaching of the inner life, and especially of the negation of self, was not what they were generally accustomed to hear from the lips of a Christian teacher, though it was exactly in line with much that was taught in their own religious books. They told me that one objection which they had toward the religion of Jesus Christ was that, as far as it had been presented to them, it seemed so exclusively objective in its testimony, and gave so little room for those deeper teachings of the subjective discipline of the spirit, which appeared to them as so all-important.

" From that conversation and from many others that I had in India, I came to the conclusion that it would be wiser if missionaries could find out the point to which God's training had led the enquiring souls around them, in order to lead them forward by those further revelations which Christ has given.

" We should seek out the Corneliuses of the world, men who have gone as far as natural religion can carry them, and whose tears and prayers have come up as a memorial before God. They are waiting for our message. They are prepared for it. They will receive it gladly. The Holy Spirit will fall on them whilst we speak : and they may be trusted to pass on the glad tidings to their kinsfolk and near friends.

" When travelling through India, I habitually asked of the missionaries, ' Do you know of a Cornelius in this district ? ' Invariably I was answered in the affirmative. Everywhere there are devout souls, who have gone as far as their opportunities allowed, and are yearning for a completer revelation, and especially for the announcement that Christ is the Wisdom and the Power of God. They are prepared like beacon-fires, which only need an illuminating and kindling spark."

VIII. SOUTH AFRICA.

Following on Mr. Meyer's visit to India his next expedition, as representing the Free Church Council, was to South Africa, for which he embarked on April 4th, 1908. This seemed to him so important that he wrote a book about it, entitled *A Winter in South Africa*. The volume is full of characteristic details of his busy mission there, during which illumination and encouragement came to many people of all the races and churches represented in that land of promise.

At Cape Town he had a great reception, and this roused much expectancy, which was not disappointed, in the subsequent visits north to Kimberley, Bloemfontein, Johannesburg and Pretoria. On the way south again, Ladysmith, with its war memories, Pietermaritzburg and Durban were visited. Between the two latter an interesting visit was sandwiched to the Annual Native Convention at Ifafa of the American Zulu Mission.

East London, Grahamstown, Queenstown and Port Elizabeth followed, and then a very memorable visit was paid to Lovedale, that great Christian Missionary Educational Settlement of the Presbyterian Church of Scotland— this is given considerable space in Mr. Meyer's book ; and the following chapter on " The Murray Family," with a portrait of Andrew Murray and brief records of visits to Stellenbosch and Wellington, with which he was associated, and of the final week in Cape Town, complete the tour.

As one result of the visit Mr. Meyer was able on his return to England to raise £1,000 to aid the Baptist Churches of South Africa in Church extension. The interest on this " F. B. Meyer Fund," together with other considerable sums raised in the country, is annually devoted to this excellent purpose.

IX. Australia.

" There is something in the wind," said Dr. Meyer to an interviewer, when he was about to set out hopefully for Australia. " At Glasgow in 1911," says a leading article in *The Australian Baptist* for June 12th, 1923, " he commissioned us to say that he expected to come to Australia next year. Many moons have waxed and waned since then, to say nothing of the Great War with its overshadowing burdens of responsibility and sorrow, but he is now in our midst, and we all rejoice."

With the Rev. Howard May as colleague, and the Rev. James Mursell as companion for the voyage, he started at the end of April, and in a series of Circular Letters to the people at Christ Church he chronicles his fortunes. In his first communication, written on May 3rd, occurs the characteristic sentence, " I have been kept very busy with my writing as I want to post several budgets at Toulon, which we reach to-morrow."

The Meyer-May Mission "For the Promotion of Christian Living " began at Perth, Western Australia, on the first day of June and continued for eleven days, and in spite of torrential rain there was not a single meeting poorly attended. Then a long railway journey brought him to Adelaide, that beautiful garden city. Here the Mission was brought into prominence by the refusal of the Anglican Bishop to allow Dr. Meyer to hold a meeting in Trinity Church, for which he had been advertised. But without any fuss Dr. Meyer went to the schoolroom. He said by way of reply that he hoped one day " to kneel before the Throne of God with a High Churchman on one side and a Quaker on the other." From here Dr. Meyer went alone, his colleague having been stricken with influenza and compelled to remain in Adelaide.

In Melbourne the meetings were phenomenal. The Archbishop (Dr. Harrington Lees) presided at the first meeting in Collins Street Independent Church, and thereafter twice a day the meetings were crowded and Dr. Meyer, in spite of his years and his physical weakness, spoke with verve and spiritual power from June 28th to July 8th, greatly helped by the presence of the Rev. James Mursell, who was in the city at the same time, having indeed had a great part in arranging the whole tour. Ballarat and Geelong were also included in the itinerary.

" I shall never forget," says Dr. Boreham of Melbourne, " meeting Dr. Meyer on his arrival in this city. I had not seen him since I was a member of his Saturday afternoon Bible Class at Aldersgate Street, thirty years before. I thought I had never beheld such a vision of venerable saintliness as he represented as he stepped from the train. It was at the beginning of July—our Australian mid-winter —and, as it happened, the week that he spent in Melbourne was the wettest, wintriest week that we had known for years. Yet, every afternoon and every evening, the great church was crowded. He looked pitifully frail as he emerged from the vestry and made his way to the seat that he occupied both when resting and speaking. Yet everybody

was electrified by the vigour with which he spoke ; and, to
this day, one often hears of the deep impressions made.
Twice during that memorable week, it was my privilege to
take tea with him. ' You must get very tired,' I remarked,
' with all this travelling and interviewing and writing and
preaching ! ' ' My dear fellow,' he replied, with his characteristic smile, ' I love it ! I love it ! ' And it was perfectly
clear that he did."

By boat from Melbourne Dr. Meyer crossed to Burnie,
Tasmania, and went on to Launceston and Hobart. Brisbane
was the next city on the programme, and the Rev. W. G.
Pope, in review of the visit, wrote words that are in measure
true of the whole Australian Mission :—

" The saints and sinners in Brisbane, Queensland,
Australia, have just enjoyed a stirring five days' visit from
London's well-known Baptist preacher—Dr. Meyer.
Travelling 600 miles by boat from Hobart to Sydney, and
then 750 miles by rail to Brisbane, without a break, was not
conducive to the rest and refreshment which an aged
gentleman of seventy-six might require for sixteen meetings
—averaging an audience of 1,000 each—for five days ; but
Dr. Meyer was more than equal to it. In spite of his frail
appearance, his vitality amazed every one. He never
seemed so happy as when, seated on the edge of a table, he
faced and addressed the great audiences that welcomed him,
and listened spellbound to his descriptive narrative messages.
Such visitors bind the hearts of the Australians more closely
to the mother country. Dr. Meyer was known by his books,
his sermons and his social activities, but now to tens of
thousands in Australia he is known as a living personality,
and the people of Queensland have fallen in love with him.
The next time our travelling Queenslanders visit London,
they will look out for him who stirred their hearts and
stimulated their love to God and man."

At Sydney, the final city to be visited, Mr. Howard May
was again able to join Dr. Meyer, and from July 29th to
August 6th the people responded warmly to the appeals of
the two visitors. Mr. May in the Welcome Meeting, held in

Christ Church on their return to England, bore witness to the wonderful way Dr. Meyer was sustained and helped all the way through, but recalled a notice in one of the newspapers of a Sunday's services, which read : " Preacher : Rev. F. B. Meyer, London's notable preacher. Anthem— ' Let not your heart be troubled.' " Dr. Meyer declared that he had talked about Christ Church all the way—" I said, that's my address—Christ Church, London—till I die."

CHAPTER TWENTY-THREE

THE LAST DAYS

IN one of the letters in an earlier chapter Dr. Meyer expressed his satisfaction in the friendship of Dr. E. Smallwood who saw him safely through his illness at Beulah Hill. During the early stages of his last illness he was equally favoured, indeed, there was no break either in the care or the regard that were given to him. The two men were joined by many bonds of understanding and helpfulness, and letters often passed between them, though only a few have been preserved. On board ship on July 29th, 1926, this :—

" MY VERY DEAR FRIEND,
    " We have enjoyed a beautiful voyage—the ocean so calm and lovely. I feel rested by it . . . Deep down in my heart there is the quiet consciousness that I am not here on my own charges, and that the dear Lord has undertaken all the responsibility . . .
    " I do often think of you, dear friend. God has joined us together in a very holy fellowship, and I should not be here to-day except that you had been sent to me. Please give my kindest remembrances to Mrs. Smallwood. With *much* love in Christ.
                            " Yours,
                                " F. B. MEYER."

On Dr. Meyer's seventy-seventh birthday Dr. Smallwood gave him that beautiful collection of extracts made by Elizabeth Waterhouse, entitled " Companions of the Way," and they each agreed to read it daily. So on January 28th, 1927, he writes :—

" MY VERY DEAR FRIEND,

    " This silence doesn't mean that I forget you. Indeed, I think of you every morning when we read the same inspiring words . . . My love.

Yrs. afft.,
" F. B. MEYER."

Not content with merely reading the daily portions, Dr. Meyer here and there annotated them. Two or three of these notes may be given. Over a prayer by Bishop Andrewes he has written on the first morning of 1928, " Deep fellowship with Christ is impossible unless you set yourself to its cultivation. Friendship cannot be made by glimpses. God must commune from off the Mercy Seat." And in the evening, over a poem by Eliza Scudder, " What a fool I have been—drawing with labour from the well, instead of nourishing my receptivity at the spring."

Beneath a verse of Coventry Patmore in which he speaks of God who goes " Straight to his homestead in the human heart," he has written—" Perhaps in all the universe none can satisfy God's yearning heart as man can. We are made in His likeness. God seeketh such."

On July 3rd, 1926, under an extract from " John Inglesant," this—" Last night I had a vision that our Lord had come literally to live in this house with me : and to find in me companionship. Behold the Tabernacle of God is with men and He will dwell with them. I said, ' What wilt Thou do when I am silently at work ? ' He replied, ' But I shall be thinking and working with you.' "

Many passages he has marked. From Arthur Christopher Benson—" The secret waits for all who can throw aside convention and insincerity, who can make the sacrifice with a humble heart, and throw themselves utterly and fearlessly into the hands of God."

This from Ralph Waldo Emerson—" A man inspires affection and honour, because he was not lying in wait for these."

And from Gerhardt Tersteegen this verse :—

> O Breath from far Eternity !
>   Breathe o'er my soul's unfertile land ;
> So shall the pine and myrtle tree
>   Spring up amid the desert sand ;
> And where thy living water flows
>   My heart shall blossom as the rose.

Two more letters to his physician may be quoted, the second somewhat fanciful :—

" *November* 10*th*, 1928.

" MY VERY DEAR LUKE,

" . . . What a dear man you have been to me.   I have needed you so much in all my difficulties, but the Lord allowed me to come into touch, and we will ask that yonder our mansions may be together.

" Yours ever affect.,

" F. B. M."

" *March* 14*th*, 1929.

" MY VERY DEAR FRIEND,

" Following out our talk this a.m. I am inextricably caught in the net of your love, and don't want to lose it yonder.   So this a.m. it has been my request to ' the Prince ' that He would allow our mansions to be simple, but situated side by side.

" I seem to understand that there have been so many arrivals lately that the angels have been set to make a new road, along the River Bank.   I said that we should really prefer this—so they are preparing two places for us."

Then with two verses from Whittier, he signs himself :—

" Yours affect., F. B. MEYER."

The other book with which he solaced his last days was " Sketches of the Quiet of the Land," by Frances Bevan.

*   *   *   *   *

On February 12th he was taken to St. Peter's Nursing Home, Streatham, and remained there five weeks under

Dr. Smallwood's care ; the latter hoped that he might be sufficiently convalescent when Dr. Poole went to America in July to take the services in Christ Church. But in spite of his joy in his doctor's visits he was eager to get better earlier, and thought that the air in Bournemouth would hasten his recovery. So he was taken there by road, and seemed to make some progress during the following week ; but then the change came that presaged the end.

Every care was given to him ; his daughter Mrs. Tatam, his Secretary Miss Hames, Sister Margaret, and the nurses ministered to him. His eldest sister, his granddaughters, Mr. Glanvill the Church Treasurer, Mr. Gamman the Secretary of the Regions Beyond Missionary Union, and others visited him ; he wrote a few postcards and dictated a number of letters. On Thursday, March 28th, the Rev. Trevor Lingley conducted a Communion Service, though Dr. Meyer, who had wonderfully retained his consciousness till within two hours of his departure, was then too weak to join it except by raising his hand two or three times, and at noon he passed over. The medical verdict is that he died of heart weakness complicated by lung trouble. In fact, he was just worn out and all his reserves were exhausted.

To a number of friends he had written messages of fare-well, just as natural in their wording as if he had been starting on one of his world journeys. The day before his death he said, " I ought to be in heaven by now. I have settled all my affairs, and there is nothing to wait for. I can't understand it." Mrs. Harriet Beecher Stowe at the end said that her boxes were packed and ready and she was only waiting for the summons. But F. B. Meyer did not wish to wait, he had never wasted time in his life and when he was ready he expected to start. He had a desire to depart and to be with Christ, which is very far better.

The London evening newspapers had but one item of news that day : " Death of F. B. Meyer," and many paused in their steps as they read. March 28th is his day. His letter to his Church reads almost like an Apostolic Epistle. He seemed to forget nothing.

" Nursing Home, Bournemouth.

March 24th, 1929.

" DEAR DR. POOLE—OFFICERS AND MEMBERS,

" I have suddenly learnt that my life is closing more rapidly than I expected. I dare not ask you to come and see me as I am kept so absolutely quiet, but I send you my love. First to the dear Pastor and his wife—who have always treated me with unsparing affection—God bless them both! I pray God also that the ministry of my friend may be increasingly evangelical and spiritual. I am so absolutely sure that the springs of religious life are ever rising where the heart is true and pure and loyal to our Lord. God bless you, my dear friend, in your earnest ministry!

" The majority of the officers were young men in my first pastorate, when we were all inspired by the spirit of self-sacrifice, intense passion for souls, and loyalty to our Church—these were the characteristics of the earliest years, and I pray God they may be a beacon star. In a very special way the officers of the Church set the pace of a Church, and their personal character becomes infused into the coming generation.

" When I think of the masses of the people around us in Lambeth, it makes one yearn to see our Church filled with such, and I am perfectly sure the throwing of the doors open to the simple Gospel service on Sunday evening would be quickly responded to by those who are outside.

" The love of God, the Grace of Christ our Lord, and the anointing, quickening and empowering grace of the Holy Spirit be with you all.

" I send my love.

" Yours affectionately,

" F. B. MEYER."

CHAPTER TWENTY-FOUR

HIS LEGACY

AFTER his death there came a pause, and while it lasts we may ask ourselves what has been bequeathed to us by him whom we have lost.

Dr. Meyer's chief legacy is the influence he has exerted on two generations which will in unguessed ways pass on to generations following. Then he has left us the rich heritage of his memory ; those who knew him will treasure the thought of his friendship, those who heard him will recall the words he spoke to them while he was yet present with them, those who only knew his name will still imagine him as one of the great heralds of the faith delivered to the saints.

His material memorial is not the cross on his grave, but Melbourne Hall in Leicester, reared for his ministry, every seat of it consecrated by the meeting of God with some human soul ; a sanctuary, like himself, unique in its architecture and in its history.

But perhaps the most evident legacy is the books he wrote, more than seventy of them in English, many translated into other languages (twenty in Swedish alone) and pamphlets enough to complete the hundred.

He will be chiefly remembered by his Bible Biographies, and it would be an interesting exercise to trace points of resemblance between him and these heroes of the past. Like Abraham in his adventure of faith ; like Jacob in his prevailing power ; like Joseph exalted in due time ; like Moses in his power of leadership ; like Joshua opening up the goodly land ; like Samuel glad to greet the Lord's

Anointed; like David preparing for the Temple; like
Elijah the prophet of fire; like Jeremiah speaking only
God's words; like John Baptist content to decrease that
Christ might increase; like Paul set free by the law of the
Spirit from the law of sin and death; like Peter making the
venture on the sea. These twelve, having written of them
all; perhaps even like Jonah, the truant prophet, of whom
he also wrote a little book.

He has told us about his own life in " The Bells of Is,"
that submerged church in the Bay of Douarnanez, just
south of Brest in Brittany; in " Reveries and Realities,"
its sequel; and in " A Winter in South Africa."

He will guide our life by the five little volumes of " The
Daily Homily," and by other books of devotion : " Through
the Bible Day by Day "; " Daily Bible Readings ";
" My Daily Prayer "; " At the Gates of the Dawn ";
" Prayers for Heart and Home," and " The Directory of
the Devout Life," explaining the Beatitudes; " The
F. B. Meyer Birthday Book," and " Golden Sayings by
F. B. Meyer."

His little books on Spiritual Living which can be slipped
into the pocket, will help us in our spare spaces : " Christian
Living," " Saved and Kept," " The Present Tenses of the
Blessed Life," " The Future Tenses," " The Shepherd
Psalm," " Calvary to Pentecost," " The Dedicated Life,"
" The Wideness of God's Mercy," " Key-Words of the Inner
Life," " The Soul's Ascent," " The Soul's Pure Intention,"
" The Soul's Wrestle with Doubt "—these twelve.

For Exposition we have : " Christ in Isaiah "; " The
Way with the Holiest—on the Epistle to the Hebrews ";
" The Prophet of Hope—Studies in Zechariah "; " The
Light and Life of Men, and Love to the Uttermost—on the
Gospel according to John "; " Tried by Fire—on the
Epistles of Peter "; " The Epistle to the Philippians ";
" The Book of Exodus "; " Devotional Commentary on
the Psalms." These nine.

For Sermons there are : " In the Beginning God ";
" Religion in Homespun "; " Through Fire and Flood ";

" A Castaway " ; " The Call and Challenge ot the Unseen " ; " For Me and Thee " ; " The Five Musts " ; " Blessed are Ye ! "

And for Essays : " Where are our Dead ? " ; " The Creed of Creeds " ; " Christian Holiness and the Conflict with Temptation " ; " Expository Preaching " ; " In Defence of the Faith " ; " Love, Courtship and Marriage " ; " Friendly Counsels " ; " Take Heart Again " ; " Jottings and Hints for Lay Preachers " ; " Life and the Way Through " ; " Cheer for Life's Pilgrimage " ; " The Basis of the Free Church Position " ; " I Promise—a Guide to Christian Endeavour " ; " Memorials of Cecil Robertson of Sianfu."

He wrote a Preface for about a score of books.

He also wrote at least thirty-five booklets for enclosing in letters which have had a phenomenal circulation, exceeding two millions : " Seven Rules for Daily Living " ; " The Filling of the Holy Spirit " ; " The First Steps into the Blessed Life " ; " The Secret of Victory over Sin " ; " Peace, Perfect Peace " ; " The Lost Chord Found " ; " Fact, Faith, Feeling " ; " The Blessed Dead " ; " Where am I Wrong ? " ; " How to Bear Sorrow " ; " Words of Help for Christian Girls " ; " Young Men, Don't Drift " ; " Seven Reasons for Baptism "; " Seven Reasons for Joining a Church " ; " Keswick, and the Convention Movement " ; " Burdens and what to do with them " ; " Not Attain but Obtain." These are still obtainable.

Some others, not reprinted, may still be had from Christ Church : " Why sign the Pledge ? " ; " The Stewardship of Money " ; " Our Bible Reading " ; " Not Eradication " ; " With Christ in Separation " ; " The Secret of Power " ; " The Secret of Guidance " ; " I had a Friend " ; " Our Pilot on the Shoreless Sea " ; " The Government on His Shoulders " ; " Keep a Sunbeam in your Face " ; " Hastening the Day of God " ; " The Vestibule of Girl Life " ; " Some of the Deeper Things " ; " What are we good for ? " ; " All Hail !—a New Year's Salutation " ; " The Chambers of the King " ; " Awake and Sing."

During his life he edited several magazines. In the Leicester days *Worship and Work*, and in the early London days the *Christian Treasury*, a sixpenny monthly. To Mr. David Williamson he said that, for his own reading, his favourite stories were *John Inglesant* and *Lorna Doone*.

In addition to the Presidential Addresses to the Baptist Union and the National Council of Free Churches mentioned in earlier pages, we find pamphlets on " Brotherhood " ; on " The Majesty of Conscience " ; on " Betterment and How to Secure It " ; on " Sunday Closing from the Brotherhood Standpoint " ; on " Sunday Games in the Parks " ; on " Vivisection " ; on " Glorified Drudgery " ; " Hints and Suggestions for Open-Air Services " ; " The Dynamic of Pentecost " ; " The True Unity of the Church " ; " The Ethics of Shopping " ; " An Open Letter to a New Convert " ; on " Russellism " ; on " Christadelphianism."

Of course, many of these volumes are, in the publisher's phrase, " out of print " ; others are still available, enough to comprise a library of devotion. Dr. Meyer was such a prolific writer and touched so many subjects that perhaps his message to his own time will scarcely appeal to the future. But the books that are ours to-day should be treasured not only as the memorial of a saintly soul but as a guide to a saintly life.

CHAPTER TWENTY-FIVE

THE FINAL TRIBUTE

THE supreme tribute to Dr. Meyer was given at noon on Wednesday, April 3rd, when Christ Church, that imposing building, so fitted for such an occasion, long before the appointed hour, was thronged with such a company of people as never had filled it before. It is indeed open to question whether such a meeting of friends on the one hand and representatives of organisations—Christian, social, philanthropic and independent—on the other, had ever gathered before.

On the previous Sunday evening, while the casket containing Dr. Meyer's body lay in his room behind the church, Dr. Poole essayed the difficult task of preaching a memorial sermon, and on the following Sunday morning, to a great congregation, he preached again, comparing his colleague to Barnabas; while on the evening of that same Sunday Dr. J. D. Jones coming from Bournemouth, and representing the Free Churches better than any other man could represent them, spoke straight to the hearts of another immense congregation.

But the final tribute was given in that wonderful hour on Wednesday morning. The bells of Lambeth Church were ringing before the service, the organ had hushed the waiting people by playing Mendelssohn's "O Rest in the Lord"; had given the throb of triumph in Handel's "I know that my Redeemer Liveth"; when the three men appointed to take the service, quietly dressed, quietly entered the church by the choir door, two of them taking seats at either end of the Communion Table, the third passing on to the pulpit.

There was no need of announcement : the people rose and sang " For ever with the Lord." The coffin lay in full view in the chancel amidst a very riot of flowers, just as he, who was such a lover of flowers, would have desired. There were no tears, no regrets, he was gone to the Lord he had loved so fervently and had so abundantly served. He was not only with the Lord, but he was at home with the Lord, less a stranger there than even he had been here. So the people sang, and meant it as they sang, " Amen, so let it be." It was well. Why should not the tired labourer go home ?

Then Dr. Fullerton stepped down to the Lectern and led the people in prayer, while they responded to each clause with the refrain, " Praise be to Thee, O Lord." The lauds and litanies had no note of mourning. And as Dr. Poole read the triumphant Scriptures which had the week before cheered the veteran in the sick-room on his way to the Father, many saints wished they were there too.

Dr. Dinsdale Young in sonorous tones recalled how William Jay at the funeral of Rowland Hill had paused at an intense moment in his discourse and pointing to the coffin had said, " There he lies, preacher once, witness now ! " Dr. Meyer, one of the great citizens of London, was witness to the Bible, to the privilege of a sanctified life, to the Second Advent of our Lord, and by his example even to old age he was a great preacher.

Nothing would have been less fitting than that the " Dead March " should have followed, and we were spared that throbbing dirge, for Dr. Meyer had specially asked that at his funeral the " Hallelujah Chorus " might take its place. And never was it more glowingly pealed out from any organ, the organist seemed himself inspired. We scarcely knew, save for the reminder amongst the flowers, whether we were in the body or out of the body. The music ceased, the congregation joined in the Nunc Dimittis, and so the Tribute ended, and Dr. Meyer passed out of Christ Church for the last time.

Outside a dozen photographers prepared pictures for the newspapers that evening and the next morning ; the carriages started, the procession formed, led by Dr. Poole and Dr. Fullerton walking bareheaded, between files of people restrained by the police, all the way to Waterloo Station.   The coffin was transferred to a special train ; some scores of friends went with it to Bournemouth, where at the grave two thousand others waited, and the Rev. Trevor H. Lingley committed the body to the grave, while Dr. Poole pronounced the final word of benediction.

And of him whose body rests there we may use the most tender words ever used about the blessed dead, words coming, of course, from the lips of Him Who knew all the secrets of death and the grave—" Now he is comforted." Amen, so let it be !

Extended references were made in the daily papers and in the weekly journals to the Homegoing of the man who had bulked so large in his day and laboured so long, not only for the Church but for the community.   People were eager to know all they could know about him ;   no word of detraction was heard ;   in his departure we learned how great a man had companied with us during the years, and though we had loved him well, we were sorry that we had not loved him more.

A month later I was asked to write the sketch of his life ; and now on July 28th, four months after the date he died, I pen these closing sentences.   The picture has grown as I have approached it.   In vision I have seen the man as I saw him first on the first Saturday evening of 1884, when he welcomed my colleague Manton Smith and me to Leicester. Then he had just begun his work at Melbourne Hall and there was no hint of the austerity of feature that afterwards distinguished him ;   that refinement came with the self-discipline of the years.

Forty-five years had elapsed when I saw him last at one of the New Year Prayer Gatherings of the Evangelical Alliance, in the Moravian Chapel in Fetter Lane, the place where Wesley was so overwhelmed by the power of God that he lay face on the floor overcome by the splendour, the place from which afterwards he led a handful of followers to form the great Methodist Church. There Meyer spoke tender words about the Bible his mother gave him, and prophetic words about the greatness of the year on which we had entered, probably greater to him than to any of the others that hung upon his words. I contrast the two pictures and cannot determine which I honour the more, the young man full of energy and enthusiasm, self-confident and eager, or the man full of years and of good works, looking longingly back and wistfully forward.

His career is without parallel in the history of the Church. Other men have lived as long : other men have travelled as far : other men have preached as often : other men have been loved as much : but none have combined all these as fully as he. So of F. B. Meyer I would say, as Virgil, in farewell, said to Dante : " Thee o'er thyself I crown and consecrate."